Praise for The Ultimate LinkedIn Sales Guide

'LinkedIn is the number 1 platform for professionals and plays a very important part in being successful and growing your career, so why not learn from the best?! Daniel is not only a great example of what success on LinkedIn looks like, he's also the best in inspiring how to become a successful social seller on LinkedIn. He takes you by the hand and makes sure you do it right during every step you take to become a successful LinkedIn social seller. I believe this book is a must-have for professionals out there who want to grow and develop themselves on this incredibly powerful platform'.

Wendy Van Gilst – Client Solutions Manager at LinkedIn

'Do yourself a favour and read Dan's book! Your future income and personal brand will thank you. Whether you're newer to LinkedIn or a seasoned pro, this book is a masterclass on social selling. All the best new tactics and strategies (backed by data) that you can easily action today.

Tired of getting ghosted? As a marketing leader, I get pitched A LOT on LinkedIn but 99% of messages get ignored. The 1% that get my attention? They follow Dan's golden rules for social selling. Now you can steal Dan's full playbook. Seriously, get it. He's unpacked all the secret sauce on how he built a raving fan base of 640,000+ and a 7-figure business using the exact same social selling tips and tricks. Get your unfair advantage on LinkedIn with Dan's new book. It's the best investment you can make in 2021'.

Mark P. Jung – Head of Marketing at Dooly.ai

"This is the book I wished I had written! In short, this is a "one stop shop" for everything you need to know about how to *really* use LinkedIn and all packaged up and delivered in Daniel's inimitable style. I picked up a lot of new tips and tricks and feel confident that anyone who implements even some of these will see an increase in their social selling KPIs'.

Shane Burchett – Channel Development Manager at Canon

'Sequels are often a disappointment, but not this one! It would be difficult to follow the ever-growing list of LinkedIn gurus and even more difficult to decipher the sometimes conflicting advice, which is why I stick with Dan.

The valuable content shared throughout this book, the first book and his LinkedIn profile is real, practical and ironically, isn't just about generating likes and shares!

There's only one thing better than reading this book, and that's hiring Dan for live training. Dan has made a difference to our ability to capitalise on LinkedIn's wealth of opportunity. Thank you Dan and keep up the incredible work'.

Luke Warren – Chief Executive Officer at Kinetic Software

'*The Ultimate LinkedIn Sales Guide* is an excellent sequel to *The Million Pound LinkedIn Message*. In his 2nd book (User's Manual) Daniel goes deeper into explaining how you can become more proficient at social selling and get more out of LinkedIn's powerful platform. Dan is an entertaining storyteller and he makes social selling easy to understand and to start doing, from how to search for high level prospects, to best practices for creating and sharing content, how to engage your target customers, build your brand, expand your network and increase sales.

We were blessed to have Dan train our international sales team back in January 2020, just before the Covid-19 pandemic hit the global economy and shut down travel and customer visits. Dan opened our eyes to all the possibilities and opportunities and he converted our team into Social Selling Evangelists. His training continues to pay off and we are generating leads and closing sales all over the world, every week, by just doing what he taught us. This book is a must read for adaptive sales leaders who want to stay relevant and who want to thrive, win and remain successful in a rapidly changing world'.

Jim Skelly – Vice President, International Sales at Cambro Manufacturing

'*The Million Pound LinkedIn Message* is the best book I've read on LinkedIn and I've read all of them. So I was excited about reading Daniel's Disney's follow-up, *The Ultimate LinkedIn Sales Guide*.

So many books are worth reading until 50 pages, then they often become repetitive. This book continues to inform, educate and give massive value to the reader and will make a difference to anyone who wants to understand how to leverage LinkedIn to build their profile and generate more sales. It's tough writing a good book. Bravo on writing two excellent books'.

Niraj Kapur – Best Selling Sales Author, Trainer & Coach

THE ULTIMATE LINKEDIN SALES GUIDE

THE ULTIMATE LINKEDIN SALES GUIDE

HOW TO USE DIGITAL AND SOCIAL SELLING TO TURN LINKEDIN INTO A LEAD, SALES AND REVENUE GENERATING MACHINE

DANIEL DISNEY

WILEY

This edition first published 2021

This work was produced in collaboration with Write Business Results Limited. For more information on Write Business Results' business book, blog, and podcast services, please visit their website: www.writebusinessresults.com, email us on info@info@writebusinessresults.com or call us on 020 3752 7057.

Registered office
John Wiley & Sons Ltd, The Atrium, Southern Gate, Chichester, West Sussex, PO19 8SQ, United Kingdom

For details of our global editorial offices, for customer services and for information about how to apply for permission to reuse the copyright material in this book please see our website at www.wiley.com.

Library of Congress Cataloging-in-Publication Data is Available

ISBN 978-1-119-78788-4 (hardback); ISBN 978-1-119-78789-1 (ePUB); ISBN 978-1-119-78790-7 (ePDF)

Cover Design: Wiley

Set in 12/18pt MinionPro by SPi Global, Chennai, India

'The question is not whether or not you should use LinkedIn, it's whether you let your competitors use it better'.

CONTENTS

CONTENTS

FOREWORD

In modern sales, an omni-channel approach to prospecting and sales engagement gives you the highest probability of reaching the right prospect, at the right time, with the right message. From the phone and email to video, direct and text messaging, and social media, B2B sales professionals have more ways to engage prospects than at any time in history.

LinkedIn, in particular, has become a crucial part of the modern B2B toolkit. For the sales profession, LinkedIn is the most important technological advancement since the telephone.

I've endured my share of salespeople who whine that they are not comfortable on social media, don't know how to use it, think it is a waste of time, and mostly complain that they don't have time for it. If you are in this camp, then you need to wake up – and fast!

There has never been a time in sales when so much information about so many buyers was this easy to access. And not just contact information, but context. Through the social channel, we gain glimpses into our prospects' behaviour, desires, preferences, and triggers that drive buying behaviour and open buying windows.

It is critical that you include LinkedIn in your sales strategy. As a sales tool, it is essential. No matter what you are selling, LinkedIn is no longer optional.

To be blunt, it is stupid to ignore LinkedIn. Pure sales malpractice. Eventually it will be a death sentence for your career.

Enter Daniel Disney, a man who lives and breathes LinkedIn. Daniel's passion and energy for LinkedIn is infectious, motivating, and present on every page. It makes this wonderful book hard to put down.

What I love most about this book is that it is short on theory and long on how-to. It is a practical deep dive into every facet of LinkedIn. Daniel teaches you exactly how to leverage and master LinkedIn for lead generation, prospecting, advancing pipeline opportunities, and elevating your personal brand.

If you are ready to master LinkedIn and gain a distinct competitive edge in the marketplace, start reading now. But, before you get started, stop and grab your highlighter. I promise you will need it.

- Jeb Blount, CEO of Sales Gravy (www.salesgravy.com) & author of *Virtual Selling: A Quick-Start Guide to Leveraging Video, Technology, and Virtual Communication Channels to Engage Remote Buyers and Close Deals Fast*

ABOUT THE AUTHOR

My name is Daniel Disney, and firstly, no, I am not related to Walt Disney (that I know of anyway).

I am on a mission to help everyone leverage LinkedIn to its full potential to grow their personal brands, grow their businesses, generate more leads and sell more.

What separates me from 99% of the LinkedIn experts and trainers out there is that I am a salesperson at heart, not a marketer.

Whilst I have learned how to generate a very large amount of consistent qualified inbound leads from LinkedIn, grow brands and reach millions of people through content, my passion and focus has always been, and will always be, selling.

Here are a few of my LinkedIn achievements:

- 70,000+ Personal LinkedIn Profile Followers
- 650,000+ LinkedIn Company Page Followers
- £Millions in Revenue from LinkedIn
- 300+ Articles Published on LinkedIn
- 150 Million+ Content Views Every Year
- 10,000+ New Followers Every Single Month
- No.1 Most Influential Sales Expert on LinkedIn 2018, 2019 and 2020

Not only have I achieved a lot on LinkedIn, but I continue to do this every single day, even as you're reading this book right now.

I leverage LinkedIn and social selling not only to sell my LinkedIn training courses and international keynote talks, but I use it to sell advertising packages for my other business, The Daily Sales. I utilise everything that you will read in this book to generate opportunities, grow relationships, close sales and manage accounts selling advertising space and media partnerships.

What you'll read in this book are tried, tested, proven and mastered techniques, strategies and tips for turning LinkedIn into a lead generating and sales closing machine.

For more information on me and what I offer, along with daily social selling, LinkedIn and sales tips, follow me on LinkedIn, Facebook, Twitter and Instagram, subscribe to my YouTube channel and check out my website –

www.danieldisney.online

MY LINKEDIN JOURNEY

I joined LinkedIn on Monday 15th October 2012 after joining a fast-growing tech business as their Regional Sales Manager. Tasked with bringing on new big accounts, I started doing what I had always done, picking up the phone and cold-calling.

One morning, a few weeks into the role, an email came through from 'LinkedIn'. The headline mentioned that someone I knew had sent me a connection request through LinkedIn. (Now, even if you don't have LinkedIn, people can add you from your email address, which in turn prompts people not using LinkedIn to create a profile.)

Curious, I took a look at this social network called LinkedIn. It didn't look like Facebook or Twitter, it was filled with professional content, people had job titles, it was like an online networking event. I set up my profile and accepted the connection request.

After struggling to get through to some of the larger companies that I was targeting, one problem kept cropping up. Every time I would get through the gatekeeper, nine times out of 10 they would only connect me to the decision maker IF I had their name. The problem was that the information I had wasn't fantastic and often didn't come with names, or where it did they were people who had left many, many years ago.

One account was really bugging me, as I had a strong feeling it would be a really good fit and a really good opportunity. So, I logged into LinkedIn and decided to search for their company page. When I scrolled around, I noticed there was a page within it that had all of their employees listed. I clicked through, scrolled around and then right there in front of my eyes was the full name of the decision maker I had been trying to reach for weeks.

Barely two to three minutes of scrolling on LinkedIn and I'd found something that I had needed for weeks, the key to get through the tough gatekeeper door. I phoned up the company, gave them the name and was connected straightaway.

This was the start of my LinkedIn journey.

After learning that particular function on LinkedIn, I then started to read the information on my prospects' profiles. Before I knew it, I was finding tons of valuable information that I could then use on sales calls and visits. The next progression was learning how to use the messaging function to start conversations with prospects and even progress/chase opportunities through the sales process. Eventually I was even closing deals through LinkedIn messages.

The next step was to start utilising content on LinkedIn. I had been reading and consuming content on LinkedIn for a long time now and loved some of the articles from thought leaders around the world. I decided it was time for me to write a LinkedIn article. This was, I believe, around 2015. I had ZERO experience in writing, I didn't study literature at university or have any experience in writing blogs. The most experience I had in writing was writing sales emails to prospects and customers!

However, I decided to give this a go. I wrote a simple article on my personal favourite motivational sales quotes. Looking back, it was pretty terrible! It had a horrible image that didn't fit the screen, the writing was all over the place and it didn't generate much more than a few likes. But at the time, I had never got 'likes' before, so a few for me was amazing!

I kept writing articles, at least one a week, and as each article went out, more people began to read them and engage with them. After a few months, I received my first inbound lead following an article I published. Someone had read my blog, viewed my profile, seen what I offered and was interested. After a few LinkedIn messages back and forth we jumped on a call, set up a meeting and they converted into a customer within a week.

After that I then went on to discover how to generate OUT-BOUND sales opportunities via LinkedIn. We will cover that more throughout the book....

INTRODUCTION

'The reality is there are many decision makers out there who HATE cold-calls and will never answer them. LinkedIn is the key to reaching them'.

I'm going to start this book with a quick story....

Not long ago I sat down with the CEO of a global multi-million manufacturing company. As with all companies, to make money they have to spend money.

They have a whole host of suppliers and are often on the look-out for new suppliers. They need suppliers for components they use for their products, the copiers they have in their offices, the stationery they use, software, the list goes on.

The CEO of this company was often the target for salespeople trying to win their business. The majority of businesses that I've worked with, or met over my career, have one sales prospecting activity at the heart of their strategy, cold-calling.

As you can imagine, this CEO received lots of cold calls to the reception each and every day. They were salespeople from a wide variety of companies and industries trying to sell a wide range of products and services.

UNFORTUNATELY, MOST OF THOSE SALESPEOPLE FAILED

Most of them never even managed to speak to this CEO.

Why is that, you ask?

Because this CEO NEVER answered cold calls. Ever.

It was not an approach they appreciated, and they had instructed the entire team to never connect a cold call through to them. The seriousness in the way they told me this, echoed by the response from the team, made me realise how true this was.

In all fairness this wasn't the first time I had heard a CEO, or C-Level decision maker, say this.

Many of them are nearly impossible to reach, many of them are not a fan of an unsolicited phone call from some salesperson trying desperately to sell them something.

WHY DO YOU THINK COLD-CALLING HAS AN AVERAGE SUCCESS RATE OF 2%?

Why do so many companies and sales teams still insist on this being the main activity for prospecting?

For a long time, this has been one of the only ways you can reach prospective customers. Until now.

BACK TO THIS STORY...

After telling me that they never, ever answer cold calls, they did admit something.

Every day, first thing in the morning between 06:00–08:00, they would spend time browsing LinkedIn, reading content, engaging with content and replying to messages. They would also spend an hour or so in the afternoon doing the same.

This is when they then told me that most of their new suppliers had come from LinkedIn.

This CEO is not alone here. There are decision makers all across the world who are more likely to talk to you and buy from you if you leverage LinkedIn correctly. They just simply prefer engaging with new salespeople and suppliers through digital and social means. They enjoy reading good content and finding good companies to work with as a result. They enjoy following key personal brands within their sector and building relationships with new suppliers from there. They enjoy researching through social media, looking at recommendations, viewing profiles to get to know salespeople and companies. This is their preference.

Whether you like it or not, whether you agree with it or not, it doesn't matter! This is the way sales is now.

For the majority of salespeople, <u>YOUR</u> prospects and customers are using LinkedIn, and if they're not using it now, there is a very high chance they will be using it in the very near future.

The question you need to ask yourself is…

WHY AREN'T YOU?

If you are, the next question is: Are you using it *properly*? Are you really using it to its full potential?

Out of all of the salespeople that I meet at companies large and small who do use LinkedIn as part of their sales strategy, most aren't using it properly or to its full potential.

Even the self-proclaimed LinkedIn gurus or team LinkedIn experts only tend to be realising around 40–50% of its real potential.

I've worked with companies that have spent money training their teams on LinkedIn, hiring external trainers, and yet they're still barely scratching the surface.

A global company that I worked with recently said this after one of my training sessions:

> *'We were generating millions in sales directly from LinkedIn; it contributed to around 70% of our total yearly sales revenue. Yet, after Daniel's training we realise we were only scratching the surface'.*

This book is designed to help salespeople of all levels learn how to turn LinkedIn into a functioning sales tool. It covers everything from your LinkedIn profile and your personal brand, to searching, connecting, messaging, content and so much more.

There is only one more question you need to answer before buying and reading this book…

Are your customers on LinkedIn?

If they are, then this book will help you leverage LinkedIn to its full potential.

If they are not using LinkedIn, then perhaps LinkedIn isn't a tool that you need to use right now. The only other question you need to think about is, are they likely to use LinkedIn in the future?

LINKEDIN/SOCIAL SELLING STATISTICS

I'm going to share with you some Social Selling statistics that have been gathered from around the world to help show you just how powerful LinkedIn and social selling is, and how you can start to use it to your advantage.

Now, we all know that statistics only represent a percentage of reality; however, they provide a very unique insight into some of the common themes and trends in the industry.

1) **90%** of decision makers NEVER answer a cold call, but **75%** of B2B buyers use social media to make purchasing decisions – LinkedIn
2) **82%** of prospects can be reached 'socially' via online networks – Inside View

3) **84%** of C-level and VP-level buyers use social media for purchasing – IDC

4) IBM increased their sales by **400%** thanks to their inbound social selling programme – HubSpot

5) **78%** of salespeople using social media perform better than their peers – Smart Insights

6) Sales teams who embrace social experience report **18%** more pipeline (volume) and **28%** velocity increase – IDC

7) Salespeople leveraging social selling experience **31%** higher ROI than those who stick to traditional tactics – HubSpot

8) **90%** of top sales professionals report that they use social selling tools – LinkedIn

9) **31%** of B2B professionals say that social selling allowed them to build deeper relationships with their clients – Inside View

10) Social sellers gain **57%** higher ROI from social selling vs **23%** using traditional (cold-calling, call lists, etc.) – Sales for Life

11) **98%** of sales reps with more than 5,000 LinkedIn connections meet or surpass their quota – Sales Benchmark Index

12) **77%** of B2B purchasers said that they would not even speak to a salesperson until they had done their own research – LinkedIn

13) Companies with consistent social selling processes are **40%** more likely to hit revenue goals than non–social sellers – Sales for Life

14) **81%** of buyers are more likely to engage with a strong, professional brand – LinkedIn

15) **62%** of employees at large companies agreed that social selling enables them to build stronger, more authentic relationships with customers and prospects – IDC

16) **93%** of sales executives have not received any formal training on social selling – Laine

The reality is simple: LinkedIn and social selling are a key part of sales now and the salespeople and sales teams that are using them are ahead of the curve.

This book will help you understand how to get more from LinkedIn; the key is to not only read it, but APPLY it.

PART 1
ABOUT LINKEDIN

'Reading gives you knowledge; applying that knowledge is how you get results'.

CHAPTER 1

THE HISTORY OF LINKEDIN

LinkedIn has well over 600,000,000 members and is growing every single day.

The network started off in the living room of co-founder Reid Hoffman (previously on the board of Google, eBay and PayPal). LinkedIn's founders were Reid Hoffman, Allen Blue, Konstantin Guericke, Eric Ly and Jean-Luc Vaillant.

Launched officially on 5th May 2003 it was mainly used for professional networking and connecting job seekers with employers. At the end of its first month of operating it had just 4,500 members. In 2004 they added a key new feature, the ability to upload your address book and invite people to connect with you. This helped boost membership to 1,217,647 members.

In 2005, they launched jobs and also paid subscriptions. As the team and platform grew, so did members, growing to just over 4,000,000. The year 2006 was the first year that LinkedIn turned a profit and was also the year that they added the recommendations feature (one of my personal favourites) and also the 'People you may know' function.

Between 2007 and 2008 membership continued to grow and reached over 33 million members. Then, in 2009, as membership grew past 55 million, Jeff Weiner joined as President and CEO. After settling in, moving into 2010 saw LinkedIn grow past 85,000,000 members, 10 office sites and over 1,000 staff.

In 2011 things started to get very serious as LinkedIn got listed on the New York Stock Exchange at a value of $45 per share. They had now grown to over 135,000,000 members. The years 2012 and 2013 saw the professional network grow even more, jumping to 186 million and then to 225 million members. When it got to 2014, they had 5,400 staff and over 300 million members.

Jumping to 2016, Microsoft acquired LinkedIn in a deal worth $26 billion with the following year seeing LinkedIn grow to 500,000,000 members.

LinkedIn is now used by job seekers looking to secure their next role, by employers searching for the best talent, salespeople trying to reach their prospects, businesses looking to reach their target audience, marketers sharing content and entrepreneurs building their brands.

It's become THE professional social network, the place where professionals can share, engage and do business. It's like attending a physical networking event, but with over 600,000,000 attendees. It allows anyone in the world access to so much opportunity through their laptop, PC or even their phone.

CHAPTER 2

LINKEDIN FREE VERSUS PREMIUM/SALES NAVIGATOR

One of the biggest questions many companies, sales leaders and salespeople ask me when using LinkedIn is: Do I need LinkedIn Sales Navigator to be good at social selling?

LinkedIn Sales Navigator, for those who don't know, is LinkedIn's premium upgraded sales option. You pay a monthly or yearly subscription fee and get access to a whole host of additional features that aren't available on the standard free LinkedIn account.

There are actually two questions that you need to ask with two very important answers:

Do you have to have LinkedIn Premium or Sales Navigator to be successful on LinkedIn in generating leads and sales?

The answer is a very strong no. No, you do not need to pay to upgrade to a premium LinkedIn account to generate leads and sales from LinkedIn.

The second question that you should ask is: Is LinkedIn Premium/Sales Navigator valuable?

The answer to this is a very strong yes. Yes, because these platforms are packed with features that offer an immense amount of value.

The key is knowing whether they are right for you and when it's the right time to use them.

This might surprise you, but most of what I have achieved over my years using LinkedIn has been done on the free account. When I say most, I mean literally 95% of what I have achieved.

The huge number of followers, the sales, the revenue, the personal brand, all done without upgrading and paying for Sales Navigator.

I'll show you exactly how I've done that in this book, and how you can use LinkedIn to its full potential with a free LinkedIn account.

As my business has grown, I utilise LinkedIn Sales Navigator (and have done for over two years now) as it helps me significantly.

Sales Navigator for many is the next step you take when you're using all of the free functions to their full potential and are ready to take it to the next stage. Sales Navigator helps make LinkedIn considerably more efficient and effective when you know what you're doing and are using it regularly and properly.

Think about it in this way ...

Most people can get fit at home; you don't need to go to a gym. You can exercise at home or in your local community and achieve great fitness goals. You can lose weight, you can build muscle, all without paying to go to the gym.

However, the gym offers many benefits. The gym has all of the great equipment to enhance that process and help you take it to the next level.

Where many people get it wrong with gym membership is they pay it, use it for a month and then never go back! They just keep paying their membership fee. The other common mistake people make is that they pay their membership and actually go to the gym, but they don't know what they're doing (I did this for many years). They jump on the variety of machines doing what they think is right, but then never seem to get as fit as the other people in the gym.

This is where the value of a personal trainer comes in, and to relate it back to LinkedIn, this is where the value in getting proper training on LinkedIn and Sales Navigator is extremely important (you've clearly got the right mindset here as you're reading this book to learn how to use LinkedIn in the best way).

After years of going to the gym but never getting the results I wanted, I started to use a personal trainer. The results I achieved in the first month were better than the results I achieved myself in nearly 10 years of going to the gym on my own.

Sales Navigator and LinkedIn Premium work when you know what you're doing and you're using all of the features (regularly and consistently).

The big mistake a lot of people make is thinking that just by clicking upgrade and paying the monthly cost, their inbox is suddenly going to burst with amazing sales leads! Sales Navigator works when YOU use it properly, and it works best when you leverage all of the free stuff first.

Personally, some of the best features that LinkedIn's Sales Navigator offers include:

– View EVERYONE who views your profile
– Perform way more searches
– Utilise advanced searching filters
– Save searches and add notes

And that's only scratching the surface; it's full of amazing features.

My advice?

Work through this book and spend the next few months mastering LinkedIn's free features. When LinkedIn and social selling become a regular part of your sales and business routine, and when you are starting to hit some of the free limits, that's a good time to look at whether upgrading is valuable to you.

At the end of the book there will be a bonus chapter on Sales Navigator where I will share some of my top tips and some of the best ways you can leverage it, so if you're not using it now and would like to know more about it, have a read so you can see what it can be used for.

CHAPTER 3

THE PILLARS OF LINKEDIN SUCCESS

There are so many components to LinkedIn, many that most people never even think about or do anything with, that it takes a while to go through all of the key parts.

Your profile can be broken down into micro-sections. There are many different search techniques to find prospects, messaging styles, content strategies, and personal branding principles, which means it's a complex process to get the most out of LinkedIn.

To make this as simple as possible, I've broken it down and simplified it into these five key pillars:

1) Profile
2) Network
3) Messaging
4) Content
5) Personal Brand

Not only are these the key pillars of LinkedIn success, but they're also in the order in which I would recommend that you work on them (which is also how this book is structured). The reason that the order is important is due to how they are all so closely connected.

For example:

Your LinkedIn profile is the first thing to work on and in my opinion is the foundation of all success on LinkedIn. You could read this book, skip the first two pillars and jump straight into content. Let's say you read everything I've shared about creating amazing content on LinkedIn and creating viral content and you go out and create a fantastic post that goes viral straightaway! You're feeling pretty happy with yourself; your post starts clocking above 100,000 views.

A large percentage of those people, having enjoyed this amazing post that you've created, are now going to want to learn more about you. What is the best way they can do that? Look at your LinkedIn profile of course!

But you haven't updated your profile.

It doesn't have a background image, your summary is just one paragraph long and doesn't mention anything about the product or service that you offer now, it simply summarises how great you are. There's not much information in there and as people read through it, they don't actually know what you do, what you offer or how it can help them.

So like water pouring into a bucket full of holes, all of those people just wash away, leaving your profile with an interest in buying from you or even worse, leaving your profile with an interest in the product that you sell, but not realising that you sell it.

Had you updated your profile first, you could have ended up generating some great business from that post, which is why they go in this particular order and why I would suggest following this book in the way that I've structured it.

My goal is to help YOU generate leads and sales from LinkedIn and I'm working as hard as I can to make sure this book is built and structured to do just that.

I'm going to start by showing you how to create the ultimate LinkedIn profile, one that will help you convert the people viewing it into prospects, leads and customers.

Then I'll show you how to grow a valuable network of prospects, customers and peers. Your network is your net worth and I'm going to help you build a very valuable one.

After that we will cover how to turn your network into leads and sales opportunities through effective messaging. I'm not talking spammy sales-pitch messages, but well-crafted conversation-starting messages.

Next I'll show you how to create super-engaging content on LinkedIn that provides value to your prospects, generates leads and builds trust.

Finally, we'll cover your personal brand, and how you can become a trusted and respected figure in your industry.

PART 2
THE PERFECT PROFILE

'Your LinkedIn profile is like your own personal website. Your prospects and customers will be viewing it and it will influence whether or not they buy from you'.

CHAPTER 4

CREATING A FULLY OPTIMISED LINKEDIN PROFILE

Your LinkedIn profile can help you generate both inbound and outbound sales opportunities.

Done right, and with the right information and wording, your profile can generate inbound sales inquiries.

People will find your profile from a variety of means (your content, looking at your company page, tagging). After reading your well-written profile, if it connects with them and they are interested in what you sell, they will contact you, either by LinkedIn message or whichever other options you provide.

If you follow my advice on how to design a fully optimised profile and back it up with content and building a personal brand, you'll be in a good position to start generating regular inbound leads.

However, LinkedIn also gives you an opportunity to generate OUTBOUND sales opportunities. For everyone working in sales, this is important for you. Your job is to sell! Whilst everyone in sales loves a good inbound lead, our job in sales is to go out there and CREATE opportunities.

One of the ways in which you can do this on LinkedIn is to message people who view your profile. It's one of the best features on LinkedIn and is available on both the free account and the paid upgraded Premium or Sales Navigator account.

It's also worth noting that on the free LinkedIn account you can only see the most recent three or four people who have viewed your profile. As you start to check regularly, as long as you check this two or three times per day, you should be able to see everyone who has viewed your profile that day. As you start to increase your use of LinkedIn, grow your network, share content and start building your personal brand, you'll start to direct a lot more traffic to your profile.

Along with a few other key reasons, this is where I would then recommend looking at the paid upgrades on LinkedIn, which allow you to see everyone who has viewed your profile, not just the most recent few.

I'm going to share a real story of how a simple view of my LinkedIn profile helped me generate a fantastic, six-figure B2B sale....

One day whilst doing my daily prospecting on LinkedIn, I noticed the CEO and Sales Director of a company had viewed my LinkedIn profile earlier in the day.

It had been three hours since they had viewed my profile to when I checked.

During those three hours there had been absolutely no messages asking me for information, no phone calls, no emails. They had just simply viewed my profile.

(What I later found out had happened was that during their regular monthly 1-2-1 between the Sales Director and the CEO, the topic of LinkedIn had come up. The Sales Director had been following me on LinkedIn for a while and mentioned some of my content that got them thinking about whether they could get more from LinkedIn as a sales tool. They both pulled up my profile on their phones, discussed it briefly and then continued the 1-2-1.

As with most conversations like this, it was pinned to the wall along with many other thoughts, ideas and initiatives, with the conversation then focusing on the more urgent matters that needed addressing. Perhaps they would have messaged me later that day, perhaps later that week, maybe later that month, or maybe never at all. How many conversations like this do we have that we never action?)

As I was scrolling through my profile views, I noticed they were both from the same company, so I looked the company up. It matched my target customer for LinkedIn/social selling training.

I then used this opportunity to send them both a message.

Now, what I didn't do was send a spammy sales message desperately pitching my product or service, nor did I send a spammy message with a link to my online calendar! (We'll cover this in more depth in the messaging chapter of this book!)

This is the exact message that I sent ...

Hi (name),

Thank you for checking out my profile today. I'd love to know how your company is currently using LinkedIn to sell?

Kind Regards,

Dan

Simple, personal and relevant. Within five minutes I received a reply from the CEO. It read:

Hi Dan,

Thank you for your message. Funnily enough, we were just talking about this today. We're using LinkedIn quite a lot, but we're keen to see if there is more we can do with it. Could you please arrange a call with (name), my Sales Director?

Kind Regards,

CEO

I was then able to arrange a phone call with the Sales Director the next day.

After that, there were several more phone calls, two emails, two face-to-face meetings, and lunch before I was able to secure a training and support deal with them. Not only that, but following a successful delivery of training a few weeks later, they also sent several great referrals my way, 75% booking within the following three-month period.

A single profile view that generated six figures in revenue.

A single profile view that, had it been ignored, may have resulted in ZERO revenue.

Now, of course, I could have left it to chance.

Perhaps THEY would have called me or emailed me. But, perhaps they wouldn't. We all know what it's like in the real world, we have conversations, discuss ideas and then get distracted by everything else that is happening.

It is also very important to realise that had my profile not been fully optimised and properly designed, there is a very high chance that they wouldn't have replied to my message. If they had looked at my profile and it in no way showed me as a credible person within the LinkedIn training world, they would have moved on and probably looked at other people. This is why it's important to first make sure your profile is optimised and well designed, and then look at your outbound LinkedIn strategy and include profile views as part of that.

The question many salespeople and sales leaders need to ask is, should salespeople leave opportunities to chance?

Or take control?

In my experience, and in my opinion, real salespeople go out and hunt for opportunities; they don't sit around waiting for them.

Have a little think about how many people have viewed your profile over the last few days, weeks, months, maybe even years, which you never checked. How many of those may have been potential prospects? How many of them might have replied to you had you messaged them?

You can't change the past, but by hopefully seeing the opportunity there you'll be able to impact the future. Read through this chapter and then go and update your profile first. Once you've done that, make sure you're checking your profile views on a regular basis; build it into your daily routine and make it a part of your outbound sales strategy.

CHAPTER 5

YOUR DIGITAL SUIT OR DRESS...

Sales professionals and sales leaders spend a lot of money to look as professional as possible. In fact, anyone looking to professionally impress someone will make a significant effort to look as smart as possible to make sure they make a good impression.

Men will spend lots of money buying suits, shirts, ties, shoes, accessories, etc., women will spend lots on dresses, blouses, suits, smart wear, shoes, accessories, etc., all to make sure they look as smart as possible in front of their prospects and customers.

They do this to make the strongest possible first impression and to ensure that they build and maintain trust and respect from their prospects and customers alike.

After all, if you were about to meet a valuable prospect, someone you were hoping would buy from you in the near future, would you go dressed in a tracksuit?

The reality for many of you reading this book is that the first impression you'll actually make won't be physical, but digital. For many of you, the first impression that your prospects will have of you is what they see when they visit your LinkedIn profile.

This has been the reality for years and yet most salespeople don't think about this or do anything to control this situation.

You no longer just have to be smart and presentable physically; you now have to do it digitally as well.

The question you need to ask yourself right now is …

If my prospect viewed my LinkedIn profile right now, what would they think?

Would they think, 'Wow. this person looks smart, professional and trustworthy', or would they think, 'Oh, look, it's just another salesperson'?

You want them to be impressed or intrigued. This is what I will help you achieve in this chapter.

The first thing I will do when I'm training a sales team or business on LinkedIn is a full team profile audit. My complete checklist is a bit longer and slightly more complex, but here is a good starting point to see how your profile currently rates in its optimisation:

☐ Do you have a professionally taken headshot?

☐ Do you have a professionally created LinkedIn banner that tells people what you do in an engaging way?

☐ Does your headline tell people what it is that you do?

☐ Is your profile summary close to the 2,000-character limit?

☐ Is your profile summary focused on your ideal customer and not on you?

☐ Does your profile summary have your contact details included?

☐ Does your profile summary have strong relevant media attached to it?

☐ Are your skills listed to include the most relevant ones in your top three?

☐ Do you have more than five recommendations on your LinkedIn profile?

Seventy to 80% of people that I train have none of those things, with a small percentage having four or five of them. I can count on one hand how many people I've met that have had all of them ticked.

80% THOUGHT THEIR PROFILE WAS ALREADY GOOD ENOUGH

During one of my corporate training sessions recently, before I taught them how to optimise their profiles, I asked the group how many thought their LinkedIn profile was good. Eighty per cent of the group said they thought that theirs was currently good.

After I delivered the profile training, I asked the same group the same question: Do you think your current profile is good enough?

Eighty per cent said no, it wasn't.

By the end of this chapter you'll know exactly what you need to do to fully optimise your LinkedIn profile. When you've applied my advice, you'll be able to tick all of those boxes and more.

Once you've optimised your LinkedIn profile, the next thing you want to start doing is looking at WHO is viewing it …

One of the most amazing features on LinkedIn (and it's one of the free features) is that you can SEE who is viewing your LinkedIn profile.

On a free LinkedIn account you can only see the most recent four people who have viewed your profile.

If you are new to using LinkedIn consistently, this should be more than enough for you for the first few months. However, once you start to grow your audience and connect to people on a larger scale, this is one of the features of LinkedIn Premium or Sales Navigator that really justifies the cost. With upgraded accounts you can see EVERYONE who has viewed your profile, which holds a lot of business and sales potential.

A percentage of people viewing your profile will be potential prospects. They will be drawn to your profile by searching for your product or service, by hearing your name from someone, by being referred to you, by coming across your content or your personal brand. They may then find you on LinkedIn and read your profile (which is why it is so important that you have the best possible profile!).

STEP 1 Check your profile views two or three times per day. This is only a two to three-minute task. Go to your profile, click 'who's viewed my profile' and look at the most recent people to have viewed it. I'd recommend checking it first thing in the morning when you arrive to work or get to your desk. I'd then recommend checking it before or during lunch, and finally one last check at the end of the day before you're due to finish work.

STEP 2 Qualify those people viewing your profile; if they tick enough boxes and you believe there is potential there, move onto Step 3. If you don't think there is any potential, think about whether they may know anyone who may be a prospect or customer, and whether it is worth reaching out to them and starting a conversation. If not, then just move on. It will become physically impossible to talk to everyone who views your profile and who you're connected with, so make sure your time is invested in people that have the potential to help you get to a sale.

STEP 3 If you're confident or part-confident that they may be a potential prospect, now is the time to look at the best ways to approach them. Like the example above, one of the best ways is to simply message them, thanking them for viewing your profile and asking them something relevant to their role or the product/service that you offer and how they're currently utilising that.

STEP 4 If there's an interest, GREAT! Well done, now the goal is to get them into a place where you can have a more thorough conversation to identify needs and finally create a sales lead or opportunity. This might be via email, a phone call, a Skype, Zoom or even a face-to-face meeting.

STEP 5 Rinse and repeat. Keeping checking those views every single day. Just remember, if you miss a day, you might miss someone viewing your profile who could be your biggest opportunity to date! By missing that view and not acting on it, they may have looked at one of your competitors' profiles and ended up speaking to them instead.

Own your profile views, keep on top of them and make this a solid part of your sales day alongside all your other key sales activities.

CHAPTER 6

COMMON LINKEDIN PROFILE MISTAKES

Before I talk you through how to build the ultimate LinkedIn profile, I just want to highlight some of the common mistakes that I often see.

POOR PROFILE PICTURE

Back when I first joined LinkedIn in 2012, it was hard to get a good LinkedIn photo!

Mobile phones didn't have the types of cameras that they do now and professional photographers weren't offering LinkedIn photo shoots. Because of this, a lot of people looked through their photo folder or through their Facebook photos and tried to find the most professional looking photo (nine times out of 10 this was a photo from the last wedding they attended!).

I've seen everything from wedding photos and photos of people at the beach, to one of the worst (and unfortunately also quite common) – a picture of someone holding a pint of beer! Now don't get me wrong, if they are selling beer, then that might work, but most of the time they aren't.

NO BACKGROUND/BANNER IMAGE

Possibly one of the biggest mistakes and a huge missed opportunity is not having any background behind your profile photo. Again, when I first joined LinkedIn the only way you could get a good LinkedIn background was to pay for LinkedIn Premium. Now, however, it is super-easy to do (I'll show you just how easy in this chapter).

WEAK OR NO SUMMARY

If you only have one or two paragraphs as your summary, again you are missing out. There is a lot more room for text and the opportunity for you to include some key information that, when written in the right way, can help dramatically increase your inbound and outbound sales opportunities.

THE SALESPERSON SUMMARY

A big trap for many salespeople is to write their summary as if they're applying for a job. This often involves writing about how amazing they are at selling, how many times they've 'smashed' their sales target, how many times they hit presidents club etc.

To a recruiter this may look amazing, but to a prospect or customer this tells them one thing: that you're only after one thing!

ZERO RECOMMENDATIONS

It always amazes me how many people don't have any recommendations on their profile. This is one of the strongest features of your LinkedIn profile and one of most relevant parts right now. They're easy to gain and can unlock so many potential opportunities.

CREATING A CUSTOMER-FOCUSED LINKEDIN PROFILE

A common trap that a lot of people fall into is that they design their LinkedIn profile like an online CV.

This is completely understandable, though; the layout of the profile is nearly identical to a CV! Don't get me wrong, if you are trying to get a job, then of course, 100% your profile should look and read like a digital CV (LinkedIn is one of the best platforms for getting a job).

If, however, you want to leverage it to generate sales (which I'm guessing you do as you are reading this book!), then you do not want a CV profile. You are not trying to get hired by your prospect, you want them to buy from you. There is a big difference in how a CV profile looks to how a sales professional's profile looks.

For example:

If you want to get a job in sales, you'll need to showcase your achievements. How many times have you beaten your target, what did you beat it by, have you ever achieved presidents club, what percentage did you beat your quota by, what experience in selling do you have, etc.

That information is crucial and very valuable in securing a good sales job interview.

If you're trying to build trust with a prospect, it can have the complete opposite effect!

Boasting about how great a salesperson you are isn't going to impress your prospects or build any trust. Chances are it will scare them away as you appear to be more interested in selling than helping them.

This is why it's important to redesign your LinkedIn profile to become customer focused, and not sales focused. Your profile shouldn't be about how great you are but about how you can help them.

CHAPTER 7

BUILDING THE ULTIMATE LINKEDIN PROFILE

Let's dive straight into how you can build the ultimate customer-focused LinkedIn profile designed to help you sell.

LINKEDIN PROFILE URL

Character Limit – 30

Whenever you first joined LinkedIn, they would have created a unique web address for your individual profile. It's normally something like www.linkedin.com/in/d234f87hgsn820 (a random collection of letters and numbers). The first thing I would recommend doing is customizing this, so it looks more professional when people view your profile.

When you go onto your profile on LinkedIn, you'll see in the top right-hand corner the option to 'Edit public profile & URL'. Click on that and on the next page, in the same spot in the top right-hand corner, you'll see the option to 'Edit your custom URL'.

What I would recommend is then deleting the random letters and numbers and changing it to your name, or your name and business. Mine is http://www.linkedin.com/in/danieldisney.

LINKEDIN PROFILE PHOTO

Recommended Photo Size – 400 X 400

LinkedIn profiles with photos get 21x more views and 36x more messages.

(Source: LinkedIn)

The first place I'd recommend starting is with your profile photo. This is often the first thing that will be noticed on your profile, which means it has a big impact on the first impression that you make. I mentioned earlier some of the common mistakes people make when choosing a profile photo, the wedding photo being the most common!

Several years ago, it was really difficult to get a good profile photo, but right now, in 2020 and beyond, it has never been easier.

The best option that I would recommend is to get a professional headshot photo taken. Having a professional photographer guide you to the right angle, bring proper lighting equipment and proper backgrounds will always create the best possible photo.

*If you're based in the UK, I'd highly recommend '**Shoot Me Now**'. David Green is their extremely talented professional photographer and is the man behind my profile photo on LinkedIn right now.*

www.shootmenow.co.uk

LINKEDIN PROFILES WITH PROFESSIONAL HEADSHOTS GET 14X MORE PROFILE VIEWS (SOURCE: LINKEDIN)

Many professional or headshot photographers offer LinkedIn packages, and the cost is often very reasonable. Again, think about how much you have spent on your work clothes; the cost of a professional photo will rarely be anything similar to that, yet is equally as important.

If you can't afford it, however, another option is to look at local or regional trade shows and events. There are now a lot of companies who will bring a professional photographer with them and offer free LinkedIn headshots in exchange for your details and the option to send marketing emails to you. A few emails into your inbox is a pretty fair exchange for a professional headshot.

The next best option that I would recommend, and this works very well, is to take a photo (or get a friend/colleague to take a photo) on a phone. Most phones these days have super-powerful cameras that take amazing photos.

My advice is to find a plain-coloured wall somewhere that is super-well-lit (ideally with natural lighting) and to get some-one to stand a few feet away from you and take a nice headshot (shoulders and above).

Whilst this will not be as good as having a professional photog-rapher do it, I'm confident it will probably be better than the photo you selected from your cousin's wedding last year!

PROFILE PHOTO TIPS

- Have a plain background behind you. This will amplify you, whereas a cluttered background will distract the viewer from you. If possible, have the colour of the photo background match the colour of your LinkedIn background, which we will cover in the next section.
- The photo should be of your shoulders and above.
- Ideally you should be looking at the camera and smiling.
- Aim to have your face taking up at least 60% of the frame.
- Dress in the sort of clothes you wear at work.

LINKEDIN BACKGROUND/BANNER IMAGE

Recommended Image Size – 1584 x 396

Behind your profile photo sits your LinkedIn background/banner, which is one of the most under-used parts of LinkedIn profiles.

It's an amazing bit of space that I like to call your own personal billboard. It's your opportunity to help show people what it is that you do and how you might be able to help them.

Similar to your profile photo, this used to be very difficult to do. Only if you paid for LinkedIn's Premium version would you get a set of template backgrounds that you could use to make your profile stronger. Now, however, it is super-easy to create amazing LinkedIn backgrounds that bring your profile to life.

For the last couple of years I have personally used a platform called Canva (www.canva.com). It's completely free, although it does have a paid upgrade option with some pretty good features. I've built my backgrounds over the last few years on the free account.

Canva has predesigned templates for LinkedIn banners plus the option to create them from scratch, where you can choose the colour, add your logo and any relevant photos and as well as text.

Remember, the focus of this isn't to push what you sell, but to show people how you might be able to help them. I'd recommend having a photo of your product (if it is a physical product) or your company logo, followed by as few words as possible to showcase what you offer, like this:

One thing that I think works really well if you work with a team of people, not just in sales, is where ALL the profiles have the same background/photo style. This creates a social uniform.

Let's say that I had a team of people or ran a business with people in different departments. I would encourage everyone to have the same red background/banner image and the same style of profile photo, ideally taken by the same professional photographer, with the same red colour behind it.

(Check out the team at Gong.io who bring this to life.)

For anyone looking to take their profile to the next level, there are now companies offering professionally designed LinkedIn profile banners. I used the 'LinkedIn Banner Boy' Jack Bainbridge to design mine and he was able to design something that I'd never be able to do myself. A small investment for a very important part of social selling. Email hello@iamproductionsgroup.com for more information on their LinkedIn services.

LINKEDIN NAME AND HEADLINE

LinkedIn Name

Character Limit – First Name 20 characters, Last Name 40 characters

After your banner it's time to look at your name. This may sound like a weird one to have to think about, but you do have a few options.

As you'll see on my profile, I have an emoji before my name. This was added recently to test how many people were using third-party software applications to spam people on LinkedIn. These software platforms are unable to distinguish the emoji from the name, and so when a message comes through starting with 'Hi (Emoji)', you know it's not from a real person.

With regards to whether you should put an emoji in front of your name, I'd recommend doing what you feel works best for you, your personal brand and industry. For example, I've seen people who work at Hootsuite have the emoji of an owl next to their name, which is the logo for their company! Use it if it works, but don't worry if it doesn't, it makes very little difference.

Some people also choose to extend their name with a phrase or keywords relevant to what they sell. I could change mine to:

DANIEL DISNEY LINKEDIN AUTHOR, SPEAKER & TRAINER

I've tested this, and also spoken to several people who have done this, and can confirm it makes little or zero difference from a sales or personal branding perspective. Having just your name is just as successful.

LINKEDIN HEADLINE

Character Limit – 120

After your name comes your headline ...

For most people your headline is simply your job title. It could be Sales Development Rep, it could be Account Executive, VP of Sales, etc.

There are three ways you can write your headline that work.

Important

I have A/B tested all of these styles many times over the years, both on my personal profile and also with many of the companies that I work with. In my experience there is MINIMAL difference between them. I've seen each of them generate great results; my advice is to choose the one that you feel best aligns to you and your personal brand.

Style 1 – Your job title

Style 2 – We help people …

Style 3 – Bullet points

AN IMPORTANT TRUTH:

Everyone knows that you're selling something!

One of the main reasons people change their headline is to try and hide the fact that they're selling something. Well, I hate to break it to you, but it doesn't matter what your headline reads; everyone knows that you're selling something.

Having 'We help people save money with X' doesn't hide that, people don't read that and think to themselves, 'Oh, okay, this isn't a salesperson, they're not going to try and sell me anything, they're just trying to help me, I can trust them'. They just read it as, 'Okay, here's another person trying to sell X'.

Embrace the fact that you're selling something; don't try and hide it. Having 'Sales Representative' or having 'Helping people save money on X' will make very little difference.

STYLE 1 – THE JOB TITLE

In my experience this style is best to use if you are in a leadership position. For example, 'VP of Sales' carries a lot of gravity. When many people first start using LinkedIn they just go with their job title as they then identify and build their personal brand over the coming weeks and months.

STYLE 2 – WE HELP PEOPLE ...

If your solution focuses on solving one key problem, then this style can work well. For example, I could have:

'I Help Companies and Sales Teams Generate MORE Leads and Sales from LinkedIn & Social Selling'

STYLE 3 – BULLET POINTS

This is the style that I personally use, but only because I'm offering a variety of services. It's one that can work well as you build a strong personal brand in your industry. It helps you cover more than one key area of what you offer and can work well if you're selling different products or into different verticals.

LINKEDIN SUMMARY

Character Limit – 2,000

The next section to look at is your LinkedIn summary. After your photo and your background this is the next part of your profile that holds a lot of value from a lead generation and sales perspective.

If you've filled in your profile like a CV, this often reads like a 'Personal Statement' which you often have at the top of your CV. Something that describes who you are, what you're passionate about, etc. It's also often just one or two paragraphs long, ultimately creating something that's not very interesting, valuable or exciting to read.

What we're doing, though, is changing your profile from a CV style to one that's customer focused. We want your summary to not directly focus on YOU, but how you can help THEM.

You want your LinkedIn summary to focus on these key areas:

WHOM do you help?
HOW do you help?
WHAT do you help them achieve?
HOW have you helped others?
HOW could you help them?
HOW can they reach you to find out more?

You want to think about how THEY will feel when they read it. What impression will it make on them and will it make them want to get in touch with you?

By focusing on the above key points, you also start to prequalify your leads. This helps you increase the QUALITY of the leads that do come through.

Keyword Optimisation

Your prospects and customers will search for keywords on LinkedIn. If those keywords are in your summary, your profile will show up in the results; if they are not, then it won't. When writing your summary it's important to include as many as possible of the most relevant keywords to your product/service/industry.

SUMMARY STRUCTURE

I'd recommend splitting your summary into four key areas:

Section 1 – Who are you and what do you help people achieve?

Section 2 – Whom do you often help (job titles/industries) and how do you help them?

Section 3 – Whom have you helped recently and what have you helped them achieve?

Section 4 – How can they get in touch with you if it's something they'd like to learn more about?

HERE IS MY LINKEDIN SUMMARY:

I help companies, sales teams and sales leaders sell MORE with LinkedIn, it's that simple. More leads, more pipeline, more revenue, more customers and more business.

- No fluff
- No guessing
- No theory

Just pure tried, tested and proven systems, techniques, and strategies to turn LinkedIn into a lead-generating and sales machine.

WHAT HAVE I ACHIEVED?

- Over £25,000,000 in revenue earned directly from LinkedIn generated leads
- Over 600,000+ LinkedIn followers growing by 10,000 every single month
- My LinkedIn content is viewed by 10,000,000+ people every single month
- Trained over 1,500+ salespeople to sell successfully on LinkedIn
- Best-selling author of 'The Million-Pound LinkedIn Message'
- No.1 most influential sales expert on LinkedIn 2019 & 2020
- Founded The Daily Sales, LinkedIn's most popular page for salespeople

WHOM HAVE I WORKED WITH?

I work with small companies and start-ups all the way to multi-billion-dollar companies, including Canon, Amazon, Salesforce, Gong, Cambro, Novatech, Moore Stephens, Travelodge, Visualsoft, SOS Systems, Systems Technology, Alteryx, and many more.

HOW CAN I HELP YOU?

- INTERNATIONAL SALES KICK-OFF & KEYNOTE SPEAKER
- VIRTUAL SOCIAL SELLING TRAINING SESSIONS
- ONE-DAY LINKEDIN/SOCIAL SELLING BOOTCAMP
- TWO-DAY LINKEDIN/SOCIAL SELLING MASTER-CLASS
- LINKEDIN MASTERCLASS & TRAINING
- LINKEDIN CONSULTANCY & MENTORING

THE DAILY SALES

I also run The Daily Sales, LinkedIn's most popular community for salespeople and sales leaders. We have over 600,000 followers, growing every single day. We work with companies who are selling products or services to sales teams to help them reach that audience.

We offer advertisement partnership packages on a three-, six- or 12-month basis to help promote your product, service, webinar, content, or event to our large and highly active sales-focused audience.

Our partners have included Salesforce, HubSpot, Gong, VanillaSoft, Lead Forensics, Vonage, HighSpot, Outreach, Cognism, Sales Pitch Pro and many more.

If you would like to discuss any of the above in more detail, please feel free to message me on LinkedIn or contact me on:

Email: danieldisney@thedailysales.net
Twitter: @thedandisney
Website: danieldisney.online

CONTACT DETAILS

Your contact details will already be available on your LinkedIn profile, whichever ones you put in when you set your profile up. The problem is that they are hidden away in a separate section that someone would need to locate and then open up if they wanted to get hold of you. Ideally you want to make it as easy (and inviting) as possible for your prospects to reach you if they are interested.

This is why I recommend including your contact details at the bottom of your LinkedIn summary.

I'd recommend having something like this:

If you would like to have a chat about any of the above, or to see if we might be able to help you achieve (insert how you help people), then please do feel free to pop me a message on LinkedIn or reach me on:

PHONE NUMBER
EMAIL ADDRESS
WEBSITE
TWITTER HANDLE

(+ any other relevant details).

FEATURED SECTION

Underneath your LinkedIn Summary is a 'Featured' section where you're able to upload different forms of media. You can upload a choice of four things:

Posts – Show your content that's posted on LinkedIn
Articles – Show articles that you've published on LinkedIn
Links – Show links to web content (such as website-based blogs or case studies)
Media – You can upload photos, documents and presentations

The + symbol is where you can add a new featured item and the pencil symbol allows you to edit existing featured items.

This is a great way to highlight some engaging pieces of content to viewers of your profile. I'd recommend focusing on successful pieces of content that you've shared alongside testimonials and engaging product/service information sheets.

The key is to make sure it looks engaging and provides information that is helpful and valuable to your prospects whilst also highlighting you as someone credible and trustworthy. You can see in my example here I've chosen a YouTube video of me speaking at an event, followed by a photo of my one-day LinkedIn/Social Selling Masterclass. The next slide continues to promote my training but they are all visuals that help promote what I do.

LINKEDIN ARTICLES AND ACTIVITY

Scrolling down your profile, the next section you'll get to is your articles and activity section. This is simply built up of the content you create and the engagement activity you do on LinkedIn, so it's not something that you can edit as such. This section of your profile will be covered in the content section of this book.

Just to help you understand how it works, if you've published an article on LinkedIn, you'll have two sections, Articles and Activity. If you haven't published an article on LinkedIn, you will simply have two columns for your activity.

LINKEDIN WORK EXPERIENCE

This is where you will list all of your work experience to date, again very much like your CV. Whilst this section will rarely have a huge influence on generating sales, there are a few ways you can make sure it enhances your profile.

The first step is to make sure your current role has the most information. I've seen plenty of profiles where the user has more interesting and exciting information on their previous roles than their current one, directing traffic to your previous companies rather than the one that you're currently working for.

Your current role should have the most information and is best served as an extension of your LinkedIn summary. Some information might even be repeated, but it's an opportunity to reiterate the core ways in which you help people and what you do in your role to achieve that.

Personally, I would recommend keeping information about your previous roles to a bare minimum. There are two ways I would suggest doing this. One is to have no information attached to your previous roles at all. Simply your title, company name and the dates in which you worked there. This highlights your experience but doesn't take any attention away from your current role. The other option is to have your title, the company name and dates, but to also include a few bullet points for each role.

We're still using the 'customer-focused' approach here, so those bullet points aren't for you to boast about how successful you were, but about how you helped people along with maybe some examples of companies that you helped.

UPLOADING MEDIA

You can also upload media onto your work experience sections. This can include an image or document or a link to a case study or testimonial on a website.

With this there is one thing that I would highly recommend …

Only use this on your current role.

This is a great way to expand on your LinkedIn summary and include engaging media that again highlights what you offer and how you help. Adding media to a job experience will make it stand out, which is what you should want for your current role.

What might not be an ideal situation is to start making your previous roles and previous companies stand out in your profile, as this will not only draw eyes away from the relevant information around your current role, but may direct profile viewers to your previous companies and not your current one.

Here is the official guidance for uploading media onto your LinkedIn profile's work experience section:

MEDIA FILE TYPES SUPPORTED ON LINKEDIN

You can enhance your LinkedIn experience by adding and sharing media samples.

The following file formats of media samples are supported:

- Adobe PDF (.pdf)
- Microsoft PowerPoint (.ppt/.pptx)

- Microsoft Word (.doc/.docx)
- .jpg/.jpeg
- .png
- .gif – this doesn't support animation, however the first frame will be extracted

IMPORTANT:

- The file size cannot exceed 100 MB.
- The page limit is 300 pages.
- The word count limit is one million words.
- The maximum resolution for images is 36 megapixels.

LINKEDIN ENDORSEMENTS

I'd love to sit here and tell you that endorsements are super-important, that it's worth messaging everyone in your LinkedIn connections and asking them to endorse you for X, Y and Z because the people with the most endorsements get the most sales.

But that's simply not true!

Your endorsements are unfortunately worth pretty much nothing.

This is mainly thanks to them being manipulated pretty much from the start. People messaged each other requesting endorsements in exchange for endorsements, but 99% of the time not actually knowing each other or whether they deserved that endorsement.

However, they do sit on your profile and there is one good thing you can do with them. You can actually choose which three sit at the top of your skills section. Those three will be the only ones someone will see unless they open up the section to look at the rest.

Whilst they may not pay too much attention to the numbers, the words will make an impact. So what you can do is choose the three that are the most relevant to your role right now.

Simply click the pen edit icon and then click on the four lines next to the bin to move them up and down.

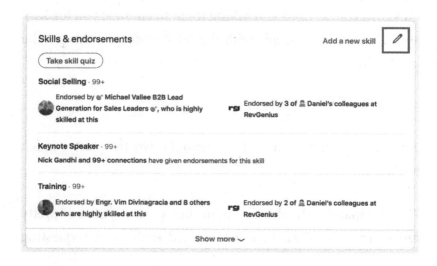

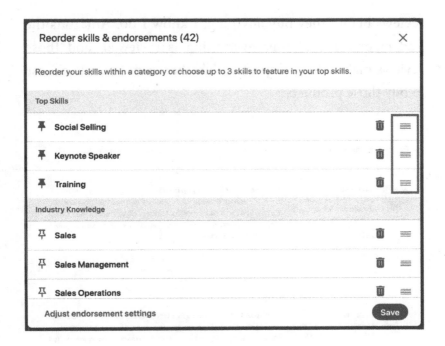

LINKEDIN SKILLS QUIZ

You can also take a quiz on LinkedIn to earn badges against your skills. This is available for technical skills, which can obviously be tested in a much clearer way compared to soft skills.

LINKEDIN RECOMMENDATIONS

This section is one of my absolute favourite parts of the LinkedIn profile, a pure-genius move by LinkedIn.

We now live in a 'review and recommendation' world. Whenever we buy online, we look for reviews. Most people read reviews before they buy anything, I know I do. Amazon's the perfect example of this: everything is reviewed, and those reviews make a huge impact on whether or not people choose to buy those products.

The fact that this is built into your LinkedIn profile is just brilliant, and something that all salespeople should leverage as much as they can.

The problem is most salespeople don't.

It's funny because it's actually quite similar to asking for a referral, which always reminds me of an amazing sales statistic.

'Ninety-one per cent of customers said they would give referrals, yet only 11% of salespeople actually ask for them'.

(Source: Dale Carnegie).

How crazy is that?

I cannot imagine it's too dissimilar for LinkedIn recommendations. Most profiles that I review either don't have any recommendations or they only have one or two.

I would highly recommend (no pun intended) that after reading this section, you go out and ask all of your existing customers for referrals. NOTE – I'd suggest sending them a personalised email, LinkedIn message or picking up the phone and calling them to ask. LinkedIn will give you the option to request a recommendation, which, whilst it does give you the opportunity to personalise the request, still comes through a little bit cold.

TWO BIRDS ...

Why not double this up with asking for a referral? After you close the deal, give them a call, pop them a message or email and say something like:

Hey John,

I'm excited to work together with you on this, if you have a spare five minutes would you possibly be able to leave me a recommendation on LinkedIn please? I'd be more than happy to do the same for you. I also wanted to see if you might know anyone who also might be interested in (product)?

Kind Regards

Dan

Assuming you've done a good job (you hopefully have done to win the deal!), chances are the customer will be more than happy to do this. Boom, you've got a lovely recommendation for your LinkedIn profile and a few referrals as well!

Content opportunity – You can also potentially use your LinkedIn recommendations as content! After you receive each one, it's obviously good manners to thank them for sending it. When you do, just add a sentence like 'Would it be okay to share your recommendation on social media?'.

To date I've never had anyone say no personally, but once they come back giving you permission, you'll then able to share it as content to your audience. Social proof is one of the most powerful tools in modern-day selling, so to be able to share someone else's confirmation that you can be trusted is a huge advantage.

Ultimately, no one will be more trustworthy than one of your happy customers. Sharing those recommendations on your feed will help show potential prospects that you're a credible sales professional.

KEEPING YOUR PROFILE UP TO DATE

After you have read this section of the book, I'd recommend implementing it as soon as possible. Maybe you want to read the whole book first and then come back, but the key is to make sure your profile is one of the first areas of LinkedIn that you work on.

It's also important to remember this isn't a one-time job. You need to keep your profile up to date on a semi-regular basis, perhaps running through it quarterly or half-yearly. The areas you should look at updating are the summary section, adding in new testimonials or customers that you're working on, rephrasing some of the sections and adding any relevant new product or service information.

Hopefully, you'll be adding new recommendations on a monthly basis, featuring as many of your new customers as recommendations as possible. Beyond that, things like your profile photo and background can stay the same for a year or two before you may wish to review them and make sure they still present you in the best way for your personal brand, role and industry.

LinkedIn Profile Checklist	
Task	**Completed**
Do you have a good LinkedIn profile photo?	
Do you have a strong LinkedIn background image that shows people what you do?	
Do you have a good LinkedIn summary that is focused on your customers?	
Do you have your contact details at the end of the summary?	
Are your top three endorsements relevant to your current role and current customers?	
Do you have LinkedIn recommendations and are you adding to them monthly?	

PART 3
GROWING YOUR NETWORK

'Master searching on LinkedIn and you will be able to find ANYONE that you want'.

CHAPTER 8

USING LINKEDIN SEARCHES

As salespeople, it is your job to find potential prospects to bring on as sales opportunities and convert. With coming up to one billion members, LinkedIn is an ocean full of fish for you to fish in. The key is to know how to fish in it effectively.

LinkedIn has built in an array of search filters and methods to help you find the best possible prospects for your product or service. In this chapter I'm going to show you all of these filters and search techniques to help you find your prospective customers.

> **Important Note:** *Before using the search techniques that you are about to learn in this chapter after you have read it, please read Chapters 9 and 10 first. I would recommend that you read this chapter (Chapter 8), Chapter 9 and Chapter 10 before applying what you learn in them as they are all connected and impact each other.*
>
> *Being able to use these search methods and filters properly is the first step in the process, but understanding how many people you should add per day and how to send effective connection requests is equally important.*

BUILDING YOUR IDEAL CUSTOMER PROFILE

To be able to get the most out of LinkedIn's search filters and features, you first need to know who you are searching for. What does your ideal customer look like?

Whilst many like to think they can or could sell to anyone and everyone, the reality for most is that we do have an ideal customer for our product or service. If you are just selling to one type of customer, this will be a little easier for you!

There will be some companies and salespeople, however, who sell to multiple industries and have a wide variety of ideal customers. My recommendation would be to create ideal customer profiles for each area that you sell into, collating the information that is needed for this chart.

The goal of this chart is to find as many keywords as possible that you will then be able to use in the variety of search methods available on LinkedIn.

The more information you put in, the more search results you'll get out!

Ideal Customer Profile Chart	
What are their job titles? E.g. Marketing Director, Marketing Manager, VP Marketing	
What department(s) do they work in? E.g. Marketing	
What size company? E.g. 1–50, 50–100	
Where are they located? E.g. Local, Regional, Global	

SEARCHING

With well over 650 million members and growing, there is a very high chance that your prospects and customers are there right now. The question is, how do you find them?

LinkedIn has a ton of search features and filters to help you find ANY prospect who has a LinkedIn profile. Once you have your search results, the next step is effectively connecting with your prospects. PLEASE read the search section first, followed by the connection section BEFORE you start using it. It's important to know how to effectively connect before you start hitting that connect button as otherwise you may miss opportunities, which I really don't want you to do! I get tons of connection requests each day, often personalised with the worst possible messages, which ultimately get declined. I'm going to show you how to find your prospects and then I'll show you some proven connection request templates that should help you increase the chance they accept.

Let's get started with the search options ...

LINKEDIN BASIC SEARCH

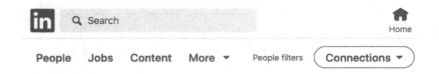

It's an easy one to start with, a LinkedIn basic search.

You simply type something into the search bar and away you go. It could be an industry type like 'Software', 'Copier' or

'Recruitment'. You could type in a specific job role if you're targeting a specific decision maker, such as 'Purchasing Manager', 'Marketing Director' or 'VP of Sales'. You could type the name of a particular company that you're trying to prospect, such as 'Apple', 'Disney' or 'McDonalds'. Or you can type in someone's name if you know exactly who it is you want to search for, such as 'John Smith' or 'Daniel Disney' ☺.

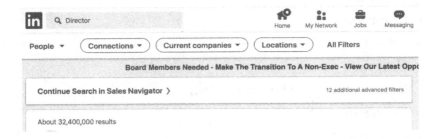

IMPORTANT NOTE – LINKEDIN SEARCH LIMITS

On the free LinkedIn account there is a search limit. You're allowed to search **1,000 profiles** or **100 pages** per month. Once you use that limit up, you won't be able to search anymore. When I was using the free account, I hit that limit pretty much every single month, and all you have to do is wait until the month restarts and search again. If you find yourself using your limit consistently, like I was, and you are utilising all of the other core areas of social selling, then I'd recommend thinking about upgrading to the Premium account, or to LinkedIn Sales Navigator. You get way more searches (2,500 profiles) along with a host of other features.

LINKEDIN FILTERED BASIC SEARCH

The next type of searching we'll cover is a filtered search. When you type something into the LinkedIn search bar, you'll be given the opportunity to filter the search. This includes:

- People
- Jobs
- Content
- Companies
- Schools
- Groups
- Connection Type (1st, 2nd or 3rd)
- Connections of
- Locations
- Current Companies
- Past Companies
- Industries
- Profile Language
- Schools
- Contact Interests
- Services
- First Name, Last Name
- Title

LINKEDIN CONTENT SEARCH

One area that very few people ever search is within LinkedIn content. Let's say you're selling into the software industry. Using some of the filters we've already looked at, you may search for Software Directors; perhaps you'll look in some of the software groups. But if you type 'software' into the search bar and then filter it by content, LinkedIn will show you all of the content that has 'software' in it.

As you scroll through the content it will present you with a few opportunities ...

Firstly, the authors of the content MIGHT be potential prospects. These are people writing about the product you sell or the industry you sell into. Check out who they are and either qualify them as a prospect (and contact them, referencing that you enjoyed their post), or discount them as a prospect and move on.

Secondly, look at the engagement that each post is generating, the LIKES and COMMENTS. Here are people who are engaging in content about the product you sell or the industry you sell into. Again, qualify them in or out as prospects.

If they qualify as prospects, send them a message. If it's appropriate, use the piece of content as a conversation starter:

'Hey John,

It looks like we both enjoyed Sarah's article about software trends in 2020, some really great insights in there. I didn't fully connect with her point about AI though, curious to know if you did?

Kind Regards,
Dan'

Lastly, you've got a list of industry-specific content that you may find value in sharing to your audience, or that might inspire you to create your own piece of content on a similar topic. There is certainly a lot of potential in LinkedIn content searches, and I'd recommend doing at least one content search on a daily basis, as new content will be appearing every day.

LINKEDIN BOOLEAN SEARCH

This is one of the strongest filtered searches around and will help you filter down to the most focused list of prospects. The LinkedIn Boolean search works around three core filters – AND, OR and NOT. It's a way of extending the search filters to get the most filtered set of results. This should be your ultimate list of prospects.

Let me give you an example:

Let's say that your ideal target customer is the VP of sales, or someone of senior sales leadership within an organisation. Here is how you could use Boolean searching to filter your results:

OR

This helps you pick up the different words that people sometimes have in their profile. Using the OR filter (the OR needs to be in capitals) allows you to widen the net when catching results. For example, you could type:

VP **OR** Director **OR** Manager
AND

You can then extend the search by adding another filter to it with AND. For example, if you were searching for a sales leader, you might want to think about other titles often used for sales, such as Business Development. For example, you could type:

(VP **OR** Director **OR** Manager) **AND** (Sales **OR** Business Development **OR** Demand Generation)

You need to separate the two filters by putting them in brackets () with AND in capitals in between them.

NOT

The final filter of Boolean searching is the NOT filter. This helps you filter out people that you are already connected with or companies that you are already working with. For example, if Microsoft were already a customer of yours, you wouldn't want them filling up your search results. Here is how you would use it:

(VP **OR** Director **OR** Manager) **AND** (Sales **OR** Business Development **OR** Demand Generation) **AND NOT** Microsoft

GHOST SEARCHES

I call this the backdoor into LinkedIn, a little-known method of searching that helps bypass some of the restrictions or challenges that you can often face when searching.

Ghost searching can help you find out who you need to speak to, it can help you find their profile on LinkedIn (even if it is hidden) and if you run out of search credits (on the free LinkedIn account you can search 1,000 profiles per month or 100 pages/Sales Navigator is 2,500 profiles), using ghost searches will still allow you to find people.

Step 1) Go to www.google.com
Step 2) Type in www.linkedin.com/
Step 3) After the /, you can insert your searches

For example, if someone wanted to find out who the owner was of The Daily Sales, they could do a ghost search like this:

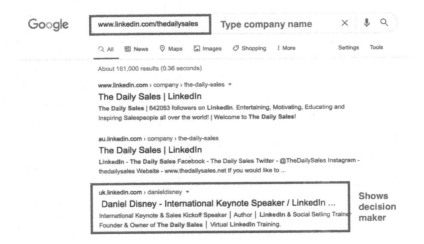

Some decision makers hide their profile on LinkedIn to avoid being sold too, no different to putting a gatekeeper on the phone to stop cold-callers getting through.

You'll either not find them through conventional searches, or as you work through a list of employees, or you'll only be able to see them as 'LinkedIn User', with no photo, title or details.

Whilst I can't guarantee that this is 100% foolproof, every time that I have used it to date it has helped me find any hidden profiles on LinkedIn. Hidden on LinkedIn, visible through ghost searching.

Again, if you've used up your search limit for the month, then searching through Google and through ghost searches will allow you to continue until your searches are reset.

CHAPTER 9

GROWING YOUR LINKEDIN NETWORK

'Your Network on LinkedIn is your Net-WORTH'.

I like to think of a network on LinkedIn like a river of fish. The question I ask salespeople is, would they rather fish in a river that only has 50 fish, or would they rather fish in a river that has 500 fish?

With the river of 50 fish, the maximum you can ever catch is 50. Whereas with the river of 500 your limit is 500.

The more fish in the river, the more you can catch, just like the more people in your LinkedIn network, the more sales opportunities you can create.

Quality versus Quantity

This is where someone usually tells me that they would rather have 50 big fish, than 500 tiny fish. That they would rather have quality over quantity. I have two answers to that:

1) Why wouldn't you want both?

    For many out there, it is possible to have a large network of high-quality people. Regardless of whether you're selling to people around the world or just a local area, you'd be surprised how many prospects are on LinkedIn.

2) Connections shouldn't just be prospects.

    This is a very important point: your connections shouldn't only be prospects. I have generated so many sales from talking to other people within prospective companies. If I'm unable to get a response from the VP of Sales, for example, sometimes I am more successful speaking to the Sales Manager first or even a Sales Rep, who then helps provide both valuable insights and information, but also introductions.

AVERAGE LINKEDIN NETWORK SIZE

After reviewing well over 2,500 LinkedIn profiles of sales-people around the world, the average network, in my experience, is around 900–1,000 connections. Some have more, some less, but the majority sit around that number.

Sure, 1,000 sounds like a big number, but that's only a fraction of the total amount of connections that each user is allowed. To put this in perspective, on Facebook you are only allowed 5,000 friends. You can only be connected directly to 5,000 people. On LinkedIn you can have a whopping 30,000 connections.

And that's only direct connections; you can have unlimited followers.

IMPORTANT – ONE CONNECTION IS NOT JUST ONE CONNECTION ...

One of the most common questions I get asked is, 'I don't want to connect with people I don't know. Should I connect with anyone or only people I've worked with?'

Here is the thing with LinkedIn, an individual connection is not just an individual connection. Every time you connect with someone you also connect with THEIR connections. If you were to connect with me, you'd be connected to my 30,000 connections and 39,000+ followers.

Back in the day, LinkedIn used to show you this on the main page. A small tab on the right-hand side would read:

'You have 5,500 connections; your total reach is 156,952'.

Whilst LinkedIn doesn't tell you that anymore, it is still very much the reality. You might look at someone and think, 'They don't look like they'll ever buy from me', but there is a good chance that they are connected to someone (or a few people) who will.

Every time that they click Like, comment on or share your content, their network sees it.

It's about finding the right balance. Obviously you can't just connect with anyone and everyone as you do have a limit, however big it may seem. But I would encourage you to make sure you have a more open mind when it comes to connecting with people. Don't just look at them as individuals; look at the network they have as well.

THERE ARE TWO WAYS TO GROW YOUR NETWORK ...

There are two ways to grow your network on LinkedIn which are actually exactly the same as the two ways you can generate leads on LinkedIn – Inbound and Outbound.

You can add your own connections on LinkedIn (outbound) and you can attract people to add you (inbound).

When you share good content, build a personal brand and engage with content in the right way, people will want to connect with you or follow you to get more value from you. (You'll find how to do this in the content and personal brand chapters of this book.)

Equally, on a regular basis, you should be adding your own people to your network as well. Prospects, new customers, other people within prospective companies, industry peers, thought leaders, anyone relevant to your role, your prospects and your industry.

DON'T TRY TO TAKE SHORTCUTS ...

It can seem like quite a daunting task, growing a LinkedIn network from 1,000 to 30,000. The temptation to want to get there quickly can mean you start looking for shortcuts or 'hacks'. I'd like to discourage you from doing these things.

Firstly, my network has been 100% organically grown, both my personal followers and the 700,000+ followers that I have on The Daily Sales. They were all grown organically – no paid ads and no third-party platforms used.

Secondly, using any platform or service to gain large followings quickly comes with a very high risk, in fact the highest risk possible. Over the last few months alone I have had several people reach out to me distraught because LinkedIn has given them LIFETIME bans.

It's understandable. A lot of the time these platforms and hacks are only used to spam-sell to people, which is not in the interest of the user on LinkedIn.

Slow and steady wins the race ...

The best way to grow a valuable network on LinkedIn is to take your time and do it with authenticity. Build a strong, credible personal brand, create and share content of value to your network and add people on a regular basis.

ADD NO MORE THAN 20–25 PEOPLE PER DAY

When adding people manually on LinkedIn, I'd personally recommend adding around 20–25 per day max. This, in my experience, should keep you under the radar and growing at a healthy rate. LinkedIn will get concerned if you're adding too many connections too soon, especially if they're not accepting quickly enough.

If a user doesn't accept your request, then LinkedIn will see it as potential spam. The more people that you're connecting with that don't accept, the more likely (in LinkedIn's eyes) that you might be a robot or planning to spam them.

HOW DO I KNOW IF THEY DON'T ACCEPT?

You can actually see all of your outstanding connection requests. Simply go into 'My Network', click on 'See All', and go to the 'Sent' tab.

This will show you all of the connection requests that you've sent that haven't been accepted yet.

YOU CAN WITHDRAW REQUESTS ...

If your list of outstanding requests is growing, I would recommend withdrawing some of them. Personally, I would consider withdrawing anyone who hasn't accepted within two to three weeks (it is very unlikely if they haven't accepted by this point that they are ever going to).

Important

When you withdraw a connection request, you cannot then re-add them for up to three weeks.

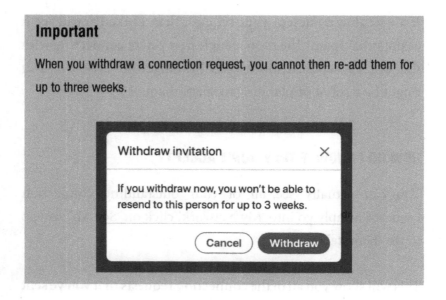

Don't panic though, this is okay.

NOTE – It's worth remembering that, just because they haven't accepted your request, it doesn't mean they don't want to connect with you! I've seen many people who simply just don't manage their connection requests very well, often racking up hundreds of requests before they actually start accepting.

So, my recommendation would be to withdraw the request, then follow their profile and use the three-week gap to engage with their content and get your name known to them in a positive way.

Don't like and comment on everything they post (that's just creepy), but every few posts click Like and add a relevant contributing comment. Then, when you add them again after those three weeks, there is a much higher chance they'll accept as they should now recognise you and after all of the positive engagement you've given them, feel more inclined to accept.

There is another option, which I'll explain in the next chapter when we look into personalised connection requests.

CHAPTER 10

SENDING PERSONALISED CONNECTION REQUESTS

Once you have done your search and found some potential connections, the next step is to connect with them. When you go onto someone's profile, you will find there are two options: connect with them or follow them.

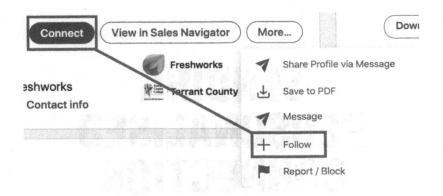

CONNECT VS. FOLLOW

Before we dive into how you can send effective connection requests, it's important to understand the two options that you have.

Follow – You can follow someone on LinkedIn, which will allow you to see everything they post/like/comment/share. They'll appear on your LinkedIn feed as if you were connected. However, you will be unable to message them directly (unless you have LinkedIn Sales Navigator and can InMail them).

Connect – This is where you will send them a connection request, and if they accept, you will be directly connected, meaning you will see everything I mentioned above, but will also have the opportunity to message them.

The ideal situation is to obviously be connected where you can then send direct messages to them. However, in my experience, sometimes the higher up the corporate chain the person is, the less likely they are to accept your connection request, no matter how well you customize it.

In those cases, following them first on LinkedIn for a couple of weeks, engaging with a few of their posts (liking and commenting on a few) and then sending a connection request can dramatically increase your chances of it being accepted.

Clicking 'Connect" and sending a request unfortunately does not mean that you're connecting with that person. First, they need to ACCEPT your request. And unfortunately, for a lot of salespeople, those requests often get declined.

The reality is (as most of us already know), no one wants to be sold to. When they see a connection request come through from a salesperson, they know that there is a high chance that if they accept, they'll be greeted by a sales pitch within five minutes.

TO CUSTOMISE OR NOT TO CUSTOMISE ...

That is the question!

There are a lot of LinkedIn 'gurus' telling people that they HAVE to customise every single connection request. The problem is, not only does that take a lot of time, but half of the customised connection requests that I get through are customised with terrible sales pitches!

Here is what I've learned over the years …

A lot of people will happily accept your connection request WITHOUT a personalised invite. Simple fact. I have the full amount of 30,000 connections (LinkedIn limits you to 30,000 connections, although you can have unlimited followers). I would say at least 75% of my connections were added without a personalised message.

HOWEVER …

Personalised connection requests do have their place when they are used correctly.

WARNING – DO NOT PERSONALISE A CONNECTION REQUEST WITH A SALES PITCH!!

It's the one thing that is actually worse than a sales pitch LinkedIn message or InMail. I will share some proven templates for sending customised connection requests later.

In my experience they work very well the higher up the chain you are connecting. Leaders, Managers, Directors, Decision Makers: if you're trying to connect with someone senior in the business, personalising (the right way) can really help increase the chance that they accept your request.

As I mentioned before, if you try to connect with someone senior without a personalised message, they'll look at your profile, see that you are a salesperson, and there will be a greater chance that they will hit DECLINE instead of ACCEPT.

CUSTOMISATION EXAMPLES

Similar to the LinkedIn message templates that I share, there is no 'one size fits all'. What I will share are a variety of proven templates that will increase the chance your request is accepted.

Template 1 – The simple request

The first template is as simple as possible, but it helps show them that you want to connect with them, and you're not just clicking Add to anyone and everyone.

> *Hi Sarah,*
>
> *I'd love to connect,*
>
> *Kind Regards,*
>
> *Dan*

The big risk when you start writing longer and more information-heavy connection requests is that they will actually make a WORSE first impression.

Template 2 – The content compliment

The next template is one of most successful, if not the most successful, out of all of these. Complimenting or referencing a piece of content that they have shared is a very powerful way of increasing the chance that they will accept.

I'd recommend adding more relevant references to the specific content piece that you're talking about, for example:

> *Hi Tony,*
>
> *I loved your video today on sales leadership. I've had a fair few bad sales managers in my career as well but thought your tips on sales leadership were spot on, especially number 3.*

I'd love to connect,

Kind Regards,

Dan

Template 3 – The recommendation

Hi Tony,

Chris Smith recommended that I reach out and connect with you on LinkedIn as he believes we may benefit from talking to each other. I'd love to connect and see if there may be ways we can work together,

Kind Regards,

Dan

This template only works if you are actually recommended by a mutual connection; it's not something you can fake. I would only send the above example if I had actually spoken to Chris first and discussed his relationship with Tony.

WHAT SHOULD YOU DO IF THEY DON'T ACCEPT YOUR REQUEST?

Another very helpful feature on LinkedIn is that you can see whether your connection request has been accepted or whether it is still pending. If it is still pending after one to two weeks, here is what I would suggest. If you go into 'My Network'...

Then into 'Manage Invitation', you'll be able to click on the 'Sent' page, which will show you all of the requests that you have sent that are still pending. You are then given the option to 'Withdraw' the invitation, which removes the connection request, taking you right back to the start line.

IMPORTANT – If you withdraw a connection request, you won't be able to resend a connection request to that particular individual for up to three weeks. I wouldn't advise you to resend an invitation straightaway; there are a few options you have that will take a week or two, so this isn't necessarily a bad thing. However, it's important that you are aware of that.

NOTE – It's worth remembering that, just because they haven't accepted your request, it doesn't mean they don't want to connect with you! I've seen many people who simply rack up hundreds of requests before they actually start accepting. It doesn't mean they DON'T want to connect with you, just that they haven't got round to working through their requests yet.

Personalising connection requests after withdrawing a connection request

As I mentioned in the previous chapter, some people may not accept or decline your connection request and you may therefore decide to withdraw it.

After you withdraw a connection request, if you do still want to connect with them (assuming they are a target prospect), you can send a personalised connection request. Here's how I would do this:

Find a mutual connection (that they actually know). Click onto their profile and just below their profile picture and title you'll see a 'Highlights' section that should have a number of mutual connections (if you have any). These are connections that you share on LinkedIn. The aim is to use that mutual connection when you resend your request, writing something like this:

'Hi John, Christopher Smith recommended that I connect with you, it would be great to connect here. Kind Regards, Dan'

Now I can't stress enough how important it is that you check first that they actually know the mutual connection. A lot of people connect with people they don't know, so whilst they may be connected with them on LinkedIn, it doesn't mean that they actually know that person. If they don't actually know that person, then sending a personalised connection request saying that they recommended you will mean nothing.

PART 4
MESSAGING

'The goal of a LinkedIn message is not to pitch a product but to start a CONVERSATION'.

CHAPTER 11

LINKEDIN MESSAGING

Messages on LinkedIn have become as valuable as a phone call or email in sales. There are now just as many decision makers responding to LinkedIn messages as there are to phone calls and emails. The conversions are often very similar; on some occasions LinkedIn messages can be even more effective.

The key is learning how to use them effectively.

For me, LinkedIn messaging has been a gamechanger. I went from spending all day making hundreds of cold calls to building a multi-touch cadence resulting in a huge increase in conversions. A big part of that was down to the amount of replies and doors that would open from LinkedIn messages.

INMAIL VS MESSAGE

For those of you who aren't sure of the difference between a LinkedIn InMail and a LinkedIn message, let me clarify for you.

A LinkedIn message is a message you send to a direct connection on LinkedIn. This is someone you have connected with, who has accepted, and who is now a first-degree connection.

> NOTE – If you are only 'Following' them on LinkedIn, whilst you will be able to see their activity, you will not be able to message them directly. This is only possible when you are connected with someone.

A LinkedIn InMail is a message sent to someone that you are NOT connected with. You can only send these with LinkedIn Premium or LinkedIn Sales Navigator.

The templates in this book are designed for LinkedIn messages, to send to people that you are directly connected with. That being said, a lot of these would work on InMail as well.

What I will say is that you will achieve a greater response by sending them to connections as a normal message compared to as an InMail.

Here is the reality that most decision makers are aware of: if someone sends you an InMail, it means they have paid money to do so. If they've paid money to do so, it's because they want something in return.

InMails can work, but in my experience their conversion is often lower than that of a cold call. I trial sending InMails and messages every year and sending messages to direct connections always outperforms, sometimes 10–15 times better than an InMail.

NO ONE LIKES SPAM

THIS IS VERY IMPORTANT! PLEASE READ!

I'm going to share with you several tried, tested and proven message templates that you can use.

What I need you to know and remember is that you still need to personalise them for each individual prospect, not spam each one out to hundreds or thousands of prospects. The templates work best if you send them to qualified prospects on an individual basis.

Spam selling really isn't a strong strategy in sales anymore, copying and pasting generic messages and sending them to all of your connections on LinkedIn will struggle to yield a positive response. What does work is sending personalised messages to relevant people.

NO ONE LIKES SPAM!

I'm sure you don't like receiving spam messages. I bet even the people SENDING the spam messages don't like receiving them!

Yet I would also bet that around 80–90% of the LinkedIn messages sent right now are considered spammy messages. (Spammy messages are sales messages sent to prospects who don't need or want your product or service, often in an aggressive or sleazy sales style.)

Their goal is simply to sell a product, which within sales in general is the wrong approach to take, let alone through LinkedIn messaging and Social Selling.

Your goal when sending a LinkedIn message shouldn't be to sell a product, it should be to start a conversation.

Please, when reading this chapter and using these templates, make sure you understand I only ever approach prospects with these message templates that I have qualified myself and am confident I can help.

Not only will you save time from sending hundreds of wasted messages, but you'll also increase your chances of conversion and success.

Let me share some of the messages that I get on a regular basis in my LinkedIn inbox!

EXAMPLES

My inbox is filled with LinkedIn messages daily and, unfortunately, 80% of them are terrible (another motivation behind writing this book!).

I'm going to share a few of them with you; I won't share who they are from, that would just be mean!

But if you read these and know deep down that you've sent ones like this, hopefully this will be an eye-opener ...

THE 'WAY TOO LONG' MESSAGE

Hi Daniel,

I trust this email finds you well. Thank you for your interest in the apprenticeship programme, I've attached some files for more information.

With the Government's introduction of new Funding Rules and no age restrictions, there has never been a better opportunity for businesses to upskill existing staff or future proof the business with an apprentice coming in at an entry or junior level position.

a registered provider of the Governments Skills Funding

With training centres in London and over 4 years' experience,

led the way in providing specialist training from SME's through to some of the best known corporate companies in the UK.

The "Copy & Paste" Email Message

New Government Funding Rules:

Under 50 Staff
Apprentice or Staff Aged 16-18 - Fully Government Funded
Apprentice or Staff Aged 19+ 90% Government Funded – 10% Employer Contribution

50 Plus Staff Apprentice or Staff Any Age - 90% Government Funded – 10% Employer Contribution

Our Curent Programme Focus

- Level 3 Digital Marketer

As you will note from the attached our training programmes start at level 3 and have the option to progress further.

Please let me know when it would be a good time to speak with you.

Kind Regards,

I have had to cut this up into three sections to be able to fit into one single slide; it was WAY too long! You can tell it's been copied and pasted from an email, which is not a strategy I would recommend at all.

LinkedIn messaging is an instant messaging platform rather than an email platform. It's designed for short conversational messages. You'll see as you read through this book that these light, conversation-starting messages work so much better than copied and pasted emails like this.

Keep them short, keep them valuable and keep them conversational.

However, they can get a little too short sometimes …

So, whilst this example was of a message that was way too long, here are a couple of examples of messages that I've received that are way too short:

THE 'WAY TOO SHORT' MESSAGE

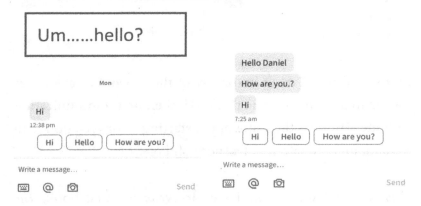

I also get messages that quite simply just say 'Hi'! Again, not a strategy I would ever recommend if you actually want to generate results from LinkedIn and social selling. In fact, I don't think I even send my friends messages like this, let alone prospects or customers.

Whilst LinkedIn messaging is a more instant-message conversational style platform, this is perhaps a little too extreme.

There are a few other examples of messages that are perhaps a little too chatty or a little too needy …

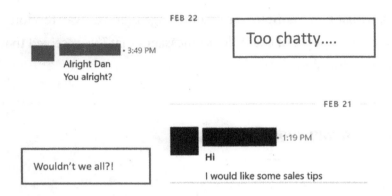

I must add that I don't know any of these people, have never spoken to them before, and that this is their first communication with me. This was their attempt at starting a conversation with me and, unfortunately, not a successful one.

This is why I was so motivated to write my first book, *The Million-Pound LinkedIn Message*. My inbox (like many others out there) is filled daily with messages like these, or very sales-driven messages.

Unfortunately, the majority of sales-driven messages are selling a product that I have no need for at all. Worse still, the salesperson could have found that out had they spent just one minute looking at my LinkedIn profile.

There is one more bad message style that is one of the worst out there right now …

I believe it's a style that has unfortunately been taught by some of the other LinkedIn/social selling experts out there, but it is one that is hated by decision-makers and one that I find quite shocking myself.

THE 'HERE'S MY CALENDAR LINK' MESSAGE

○ Mobile • 40m ago

across all the major job boards?

We have accounts with the leading sites, TotalJobs, Jobsite, Monster, Reed, CV Library, Indeed, etc, and can help you advertise across them all for cheap and gain access to their CV databases.

Let me show you how it works with a quick demo: https://calendly.com

Kind regards

Are you more important than your prospect?

This is the 'Here is my calendar link for you to book a meeting with me' message. It's one of the most ego-driven examples of selling I've seen in modern-day sales. It's very much like the cheesy, sleazy salespeople of the past.

It suggests that your time is more valuable and important than the time of your prospects, which isn't a great way to present yourself when trying to win business.

Don't get me wrong; online calendars are great! They're super-efficient and effective and make booking meetings with prospects and customers simple.

However, using them in this way isn't something I would personally recommend.

As a salesperson, you need to EARN the right to a conversation, demo or meeting.

After you've given value, built a relationship and qualified them as a prospect, then is the time that you can ask THEM if they would be happy to arrange a phone call or face-to-face meeting.

If they are happy, then you can send them a link to your calendar. Even then, though, I would still recommend asking them what dates/times work best for them. The sheer act of sending them your calendar link places value in your own time above theirs.

Only if you've gone back and forth a few times and are struggling to find a date that works for both of you does the online calendar link truly provide value in sales.

CHAPTER 12

LINKEDIN MESSAGE TEMPLATES

I'll share some of the best performing LinkedIn sales message templates that I've used over the years, and the ones that have performed best with the companies that I've worked with and trained.

THE 'HOW WE CAN HELP YOU' TEMPLATE

The first template I'll share is a direct screenshot of a message that not only got a reply, but won me a customer in less than 30 days.

This works well when you can highlight quickly how you can help them, or what's in it for them, in an attractive and engaging way. It's about trying to frame your product/service in a way that you know it's going to catch the attention of your prospect.

Here is my example:

Daniel Disney · 5:27 AM
Hi ,

I think could generate some very high traffic and leads by working with The Daily Sales. We have over 160,000 sales professionals and leaders in our network and have had great success working with Salesforce and HubSpot.

Let me know if you'd like to ever grab a coffee and discuss in more detail,

Let me break this message down into its key components and explain what made it successful:

1) Firstly, I open the message highlighting what I believe I can do for them. It's not about what I'm selling, but about what they could achieve. When I'm selling advertising packages for The Daily Sales, I'm offering the opportunity for companies to generate really high traffic and leads from advertising with us.

2) I then throw in what I call the bait, something that I know will spark their interest. For The Daily Sales, our bait is our audience and engagement. At the time of sending this message our audience was 160,000+ strong (it's now

600,000+!). For any company selling to salespeople, this is a large audience of target customers.

3) Next, I add some social proof, sharing existing customers that I know they will recognise. This provides reassurance that what I'm offering works.

4) Finally, I opt for a soft close on the message, simply stating that I am here if they are interested. Personally, I have found this style to work most effectively.

THE CASE STUDY TEMPLATE

This is another highly successful template that gets straight to the point and gives a real example of what you've been able to achieve for a similar company, making for a very compelling case.

Hi Sarah,

Last month we achieved (insert ROI) for (insert similar company) with our (insert product).

I think we might be able to do the same for you and would love to see if it's something you might be interested in exploring?

Kind Regards,

Dan

In my experience this template works best when you're selling to very senior leadership roles, C-Level and Director level, etc. The main reason for this is their time is extremely valuable and they rarely have time or interest in playing the common games in sales.

THE CONTENT COMPLIMENT TEMPLATE

One of the best performing templates I've used and seen used over the years is the content compliment. It's a great door opener. Whether you use it in a personalised LinkedIn connection request, as the first message you send or even as a follow-up message, it is proven to work very well.

Hi Chris,

I loved your post today about how sales has changed over the last 10 years, you made some brilliant points!

What do you think will happen over the next 10 years in the industry? Do you think it will continue to change?

Kind Regards,

Dan

IMPORTANT NOTE – Please make sure you are being 100% authentic with this template. You should naturally enjoy your prospect's content if it applies to your industry. Unfortunately, that doesn't stop salespeople sending messages like this when they haven't actually read the content.

THE EXPERT OPINION TEMPLATE

This template takes a slightly different angle to normal sales messages, but it opens up a whole extra layer of opportunity.

Let me show you the template before I then break it down:

Hi Joanne,

I'm writing an article on LinkedIn with the insights from five experts in the (insert industry). I'd love to include insights from you if you're able to spare a few minutes?

Kind Regards,

Dan

This template works well because firstly it creates a really soft opener for a conversation with your prospect.

Instead of the usual sales tone message, this is completely different. It compliments the prospect, saying that you see them as an expert. Anyone receiving a message like that is going to feel good!

Secondly, you're presenting the opportunity for them to get featured in a LinkedIn article. This offers a great amount of value to them. Getting featured helps boost their personal brand, gets them and their company in front of a new audience and gives them a piece of content that they can use and share.

Thirdly, it will help you gain some valuable information about your potential prospect. Obviously, your questions shouldn't be too focused on qualifying them as a prospect, but the insights that they have will often provide great sales-relevant information.

For example, let's say you're targeting Marketing Leaders (as you sell a lead generation software solution) for a marketing insights article. One of the insights you might look for is what technology and software they use currently. If you ask a prospect on a sales call, they'll often be reluctant to give you the full answer. However, in this context, their answer is for an article and so you often find they give A LOT more information.

So far you've created a great conversation opener (one which drives a very high open and respond rate). You've complimented them and made them feel good about themselves by referring to them as an expert or thought leader. You've asked them some great questions that have provided you with amazing intel that you'll be able to use in the sales process further down the line.

But that's not it ...

Once you've messaged your five prospects you now have an AMAZING piece of content to share on LinkedIn as well!!

Not only do you now have conversations going with five potential prospects, but you've got a brilliant article to share on LinkedIn that has the potential to generate more customers.

You can also directly send the article to other prospects as it will be of value to them. To take it a step further, you can send this article to potential prospects and tell them you'd love to share their insights in the next one that you write.

AUTHENTICITY REALLY IS KEY ...

I can't stress enough when using any of the templates in this book that you do so with 100% authenticity. Whenever you message a prospect on LinkedIn you should genuinely believe that you can help them with your product or service.

When you're using the expert opinion template for example, you should only do this if you are definitely going to write the article! Trying to send this out JUST to start conversations with prospects so you can pitch to them will just backfire.

With all of these templates please use them in an ethical and authentic manner. It will generate a FAR greater ROI.

CHAPTER 13

LINKEDIN AUDIO AND VIDEO MESSAGES

I want to start by saying LinkedIn video messaging and audio messaging is insanely powerful!

This is something that I would really encourage salespeople and sales teams to look into.

One of the most amazing features that LinkedIn has built in is the ability to send audio and video messages organically (not just by sending a link to another hosting platform). You can upload a video or audio message directly into a LinkedIn message and send it to prospects and customers. Best yet, it's available on the free version.

Both audio and video can generate amazing results and high response levels when done right. The beauty of both is that they take the words that you would put in a written LinkedIn message to the next level.

With audio now they get to hear your voice and your tone. Even better, with video they get to actually see you. It's the closest thing to face to face.

Let's look at some of the most important things to remember when sending audio and video messages, as well as several tried, tested and proven scripts that you can use, too.

WILL THEY WORK FOR EVERYONE?

No, of course not.

Here is the thing, some people like/love/prefer video messaging, some people like/love/prefer audio messaging, some people hate both of them.

People have different preferences; what's important in modern-day selling is that salespeople use multiple tools for a multiple-touch approach. Part of that should include trying audio and video messages.

VIDEO MESSAGES

Sending a video message is by far one of the most powerful methods of outreach. It allows you not only to send words or your voice, but also to show yourself to prospects.

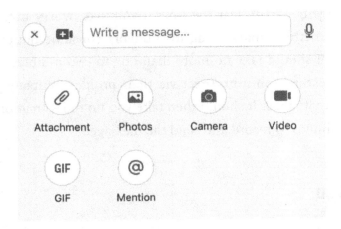

There is one very important factor in successful video messages on LinkedIn ... hyper-personalisation.

You can't just say their name at the start and then read off a script.

You need to bring as much relevant, valuable insight to the table as you can. You need to show them that you've done your homework and you truly believe that you can help them.

Hopefully, you know now that I am really against spam messaging in sales, which is important regardless of which type of message you send.

With video, though, personalisation is even more important.

Before you start to fear the time it will take, worry not. This isn't something that's going to suddenly consume hours and hours. It should take no more than one to two minutes to do some research on a prospect via their profile, company page and activity feed. It should then take you no more than one to two minutes to record and send the message.

VIDYARD

When it comes to creating hyper-personalised and super-high-quality videos, I couldn't recommend Vidyard enough. I've been using the platform for over three years now and it's helped me generate over £150,000 in revenue over the last 12 months alone.

Vidyard allows you to record normal videos, but it also allows you to record videos WHILST on another page, which could be their LinkedIn profile, website or something else.

This allows you to create the highest level of personalised sales messaging. You can show them in the video exactly what makes you believe you can help them, creating both engaging and relevant video messages.

Vidyard has a completely free version that you can use; it's what I used for the first 12–18 months. As my businesses grew and my results via video messaging grew, I upgraded to the pro account. They also have a team and enterprise version as well that comes with a ton of amazing features.

You can find out more about them here:

This then leads us nicely into tip number one for LinkedIn video messages, TIMING.

HOW LONG SHOULD A LINKEDIN VIDEO MESSAGE BE?

A successful first-touch video message on LinkedIn should be no more than one to two minutes long. You're not recording some epic speech or feature dumping on them.

The goal is to introduce yourself and let them know why you think you can help them and what you can help them achieve.

Aim for one minute and only go longer if you have some relevant and valuable insights or information to share. The focus of the majority of the call should be about them, though, not you.

It's not about your product, it's about what your product can do for them.

WHERE SHOULD I RECORD THE VIDEO?

Tip number two is also very important, and it's to make sure you are suitably presented in the video. This means that you are dressed appropriately and you are recording the video in an appropriate location.

This is often one of the areas that salespeople find most challenging when leveraging video. I'll highlight this with a quick example ...

Someone forwarded me a LinkedIn video message that had been sent to them by a recruiter trying to win their business as a potential employer.

The first thing I'll share with this story is that the person who sent me the video was actually quite impressed!

They had never received a video message before, even though they had been approached by other recruiters and sales-people on a near daily basis via cold calls, text-based messages and emails.

The fact that it was a video instantly caught their attention and encouraged them to watch it.

Unfortunately, this is where the recruiter slipped up ...

Firstly, the way they were dressed didn't quite hit the mark. Let's remember recruiters are looking for a 15–25% fee based on the salary of the employee they find. This can be tens of thousands of pounds/dollars.

For most people spending that much money, there is a level of expectation.

This recruiter, however, had chosen to record the video in some very random sports hoodie. It wasn't a company hoodie, which might be deemed acceptable, it was just a generic sports-branded hoodie. Matched with jeans and a general relaxed vibe.

NOTE – If this look is part of your brand and ethos, and you can back it up and justify it, then fine! There is nothing wrong with those clothes in principle. If you see my content, I wear either a T-shirt or hoodie, however, they are both branded and a key part of my brand image.

Unfortunately, in this case, this was quite a high-level recruiter for quite a well-respected company, where, in a normal scenario, they would have dressed smartly if they were to meet face to face with a prospect. Video is no different, you need to present yourself in the same way.

The next area that they slipped up on was their background.

I'll admit there are a lot of office spaces that simply don't have any areas set up for recording video. However, that's no excuse. If you don't have an area set up, either set one up or find somewhere suitable.

In this case the recruiter hadn't done that and had instead just rushed to record the video, choosing a very messy part of the office. There was nothing branded in the background to show what company they worked for, nor anything in the background that made them look smart, professional or credible.

When recording video, you need to LOOK SMART and find a GOOD PLACE to record the video.

A lot of these videos will be their FIRST IMPRESSION of you, so you want to make sure it's the best first impression possible. Make sure you're dressed appropriately and you find a suitable place to record videos.

When choosing somewhere to record videos, find clear or tidy areas that you can sit/stand. Ideally have some branding in the background to show where you work and to build credibility.

Lighting is super-important. If you have good natural light, then great, that will work well. If not, look to possibly invest in some lighting equipment; you can find reasonably priced desktop lights for videos on many online shops like Amazon and eBay.

What will I need?

You can record amazing videos with just your phone, and you can create amazing videos with proper equipment. Personally, I do both, depending on the prospect and style of the video I want to do.

WHAT SHOULD I SAY IN THE VIDEO?

You know how long the video should be and you know what to wear and where to record.

Next, it's time to think about and plan what you're going to say.

Having watched many videos from salespeople, this is an important thing to think about. You can't just switch your laptop or phone onto record and start rambling!

What you say in the video message will determine whether or not you get a reply, and whether or not that reply is good.

Also, just as important as 'What' you say is HOW you say it. You could be saying all the right things, but in a dull tone with no enthusiasm and barely looking at the camera. Those words lose their meaning and your video loses its appeal.

TO SCRIPT OR NOT TO SCRIPT ...

That is the question, a question and debate that has gone on in sales for many, many years. Personally, I've been on both sides. I've used scripts successfully and I've been successful without scripts.

In my experience, a balance of both is needed.

Having a guideline of what to say can be extremely helpful and beneficial in delivering the best results. Normally scripts are used for sales calls/cold calls to help salespeople make sure they cover the right information, ask the right questions and guide them through common potential objections.

The challenge is that some salespeople read scripts like a robot, bringing in no personality or charisma.

THIS IS WHERE YOU NEED TO FIND THE SWEET SPOT IN BETWEEN ...

Have bullet-point guidelines of what you need to say/ask but through good training and coaching, empower your salespeople to speak from the heart. This is the only way you'll truly connect with your prospects.

When recording video messages, having a script or guidelines can be extremely helpful. I'll be sharing some full LinkedIn video script templates in a minute, but first I'll share a quick example of what a script guideline can look like.

QUICK EXAMPLE GUIDELINE:

- Introduce yourself and where you work.
- Tell them what you think you can help them with.
- Ask what they currently use/do?
- Ask about what is working/not working?
- Explain product/solution.
- Offer a demo/trial.
- Take contact details and confirm next step.

AVOID THE 'UMS' AND 'ERMS'

One of the biggest benefits of having a script or script guideline when recording video messages is to avoid saying 'ummm' or 'ermm' too much. I've seen this too many times in LinkedIn video messages from salespeople and it really reduces the impact that the video makes. It shows a lack of confidence and often has a negative impact on results generated from them.

'Hi, erm, my name is Daniel, um, I'm just sending you a video, erm, from The Daily Sales. Erm, I just wanted to see if you had, erm ...'

However annoying and frustrating that was to read is exactly how annoying it is to hear or watch!

Yet, I see and hear salespeople (who will be the first to passionately declare how 'terrible' sales scripts are) saying way too many erms and umms in their sales calls and sales videos.

This is why it's beneficial to either create really good sales scripts or create and use a script guideline. It's also really valuable to practice and rehearse. As much as many salespeople will cringe at the thought of doing any form of role play or practice, it really will help.

Especially with video, it's a strange thing to do if you haven't done it before and you'll find that you soon slip in some erms and ums if you don't practice.

IT'S ALL ABOUT MAKING THE RIGHT IMPRESSION

You want prospects to listen to your calls or watch your LinkedIn video messages and you want them to be IMPRESSED.

You should look and sound confident.
You should look and sound enthusiastic.

There are three other super-important things to think about when recording video messages:

- **Eye contact**
- **Body language**
- **Tone**

Along with what you say it's equally important to focus on how you say it.

1. Eye contact

When recording a video, try to make sure you look into the camera as much as you can. Imagine that the camera is the prospect that you're talking to, in essence the camera is their eyes.

2. Body language

You should also be aware of your body language when recording videos. Are you sitting upright or standing upright with your back nice and straight? Do you speak with your hands? Do you look happy, comfortable and confident?

3. Tone

Finally, you should try to be aware of the tone of your voice when you record a video. If you are reading a script in a monotone style, it can come across as robotic and sales like. By sitting or standing upright you'll instantly improve your tone. Smiling a bit when you talk will improve your tone as well.

LINKEDIN VIDEO SALES SCRIPTS

Right, let's now dig into what you should say in a LinkedIn video message to a prospect.

You should have found a good spot to record your video with a suitable background. You should be dressed appropriately. You should be conscious of looking at the camera, how you sit/stand and your tone whilst speaking.

I'm going to share several LinkedIn video message sales scripts that you can use.

My recommendation is to read through them all first, then if/when you choose to use one, make sure that it is customised for the prospect you're going to send it to.

Then practice, even if it is just one practice recording. Keep recording until you get it right and you feel confident it's the right quality to send out. It's worth taking a little extra time to make sure you get it right!

LINKEDIN VIDEO MESSAGE SCRIPTS

1. The 'profile review' video

This is one of the most successful scripts that I've used and worked with other sales teams to use. The main reason for this, going back to my point at the start of this section, is the hyper-personalisation.

You utilise information in their LinkedIn profile to show how or why you believe you can help them.

IMPORTANT – Reviewing a prospect's LinkedIn profile before messaging shouldn't take more than one to two minutes. Don't waste time reading every detail, but scroll through looking for the most relevant information.

Script template

'Hi (insert name),

I was having a quick look at your profile today and noticed you are the (insert position) at (insert company)

My name is (your name) and I work at a company called (your company). We work with similar companies to yours including (insert current customers) to help them achieve (insert ROI).

After doing a little research on your company I think we might be able to help you achieve something similar.

We recently helped (insert customer) achieve (insert specific result) by doing (insert product/service example).

If you're able to spare a few minutes I'd love to show you a little more detail on what we do and learn a bit more about you to see if this is something that could work for you.

Hopefully speak soon,

(Your name)

This script is short and sweet and gets straight to the point, but it highlights that you have made some effort to research them before you approached them.

NOTE – If you can find any other relevant information in their profile, then that can be beneficial to include in this video. For example:

- A previous employer they worked for, that you worked with/for
- Something in their summary that you noticed
- Something in their interests that is relevant

Remember you want to read this in a natural way, so try not to read the words as you record. Either create some bullet points to remind you of what you need to say or practice and remember it so you can say it smoothly.

2. The 'content reference' video

This is another high-performing video script that both shows effort in your research and also uses a compliment to warm up the opening.

Firstly, you need to go onto a prospect's LinkedIn profile, scroll down to their recent activity and look for a post they've shared recently that is relevant. You're then going to reference that in the video message.

Important – When using this script, you must be 100% authentic, genuine, and sincere. When complimenting their content, you must have read it/watched it first and you should truly have enjoyed it. You can't fake this sort of style; it has to be real.

Script template

'Hi (insert name),

I really enjoyed your post (insert post topic or title) that you shared on (insert shared date).

(Explain what you liked about the post, reference key parts of the content and add your own thoughts/ideas/experiences.)

> *I noticed that you work at (insert company), which is similar to the sort of companies that we help here. We've worked with (insert customers) and we help them achieve (insert ROI) with our (insert product/service).*
>
> *I wanted to see if you would be open to seeing a little more information on our product and maybe discussing it to see if it might help you achieve (insert ROI)?*
>
> *Hope to chat soon,*
>
> *(Your name)*

The beauty of this script is that it opens with a compliment, a fully personalised compliment. It shows that you're interested in the industry, it shows that you've taken the time to consume their content and it shows that you also have an opinion on the subject.

This is such a powerful way to open a conversation with a prospect and when you then go on to discuss how you might be able to help, they will be more open to considering it.

This will work well with a piece of content that they've created within the last few days, and will work with content created up to one or two weeks ago.

If, however, they haven't posted any content for a few weeks, then you could also look to see if they have engaged in any content (likes, shares or ideally comments).

3. The 'to the point' video

This template is best used for high-level prospects, people in positions such as Director, C-Level, VP, etc.

In my experience, the higher up the chain that you are trying to prospect, the more 'to the point' your messaging should be.

IMPORTANT – Getting to the point does not mean going straight for the pitch! It means get straight to the point of what is in it for THEM. What they could achieve or how this could potentially benefit them.

Script template

Hi (insert name),

I love what you're doing at (insert company). We recently helped (insert similar company) achieve (insert result/ROI).

We did this by (briefly explain what the company did/bought and how they implemented it).

Doing just a quick bit of research, I think we could do something very similar for you. If it's something you would be interested in exploring, I'd love to discuss it in a little more detail.

If you would like, I'd love to pop over a little more information in an email that will explain a bit more about what we do and how we do it.

I hope to chat soon,

(Your name)

The key with this script is that you open it with a real example of a result that you have achieved for a similar company. I've spoken with tons of high-level decision makers and the large majority say they prefer this style of messaging.

What is important is that you make this as attractive as possible for them. What I mean by that is try to find an example, case study or testimonial that you can reference that gives the biggest impact. A huge result or a big statistic, something that will catch their attention.

Perhaps you saved 80% of a customer's costs, perhaps you increased their performance by 300%. Big bold numbers that will catch their attention and encourage them to watch until the end and hopefully reply.

LINKEDIN AUDIO MESSAGES/VOICE NOTES

These are a little different to both text-based and video-based LinkedIn messages. An audio message on LinkedIn is a lot like a voicemail.

To be successful they need to be super-short, sweet and to the point, driving a strong reason for them to reply.

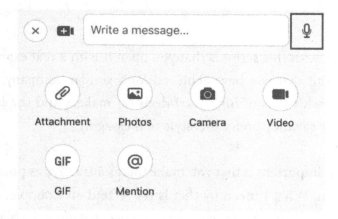

There are a few great benefits to audio messages on LinkedIn. Firstly, they cut through the noise. Ninety-nine per cent of LinkedIn messages are text-based. Audio and video messages cut right through the often-crowded inboxes.

Secondly, they add voice to what you're saying. With a text-based message, you are sending words. With audio you add not only your voice, but also tone and you start to build on the personality that is conveyed.

I've found voice notes to be effective at multiple stages of the sales cycle. They can work as great prospecting/conversation starting messages. They can also work great as relationship building messages, and also effective as follow-up messages and chasing messages.

It's important to treat them the same way you would treat a phone call, ie:

- Smile while you're speaking to elevate your voice and tone.
- Be confident and positive.
- Know what you're going to say and what you want the next step to be for them.

Here are a few little LinkedIn audio template scripts to get you started:

Audio message template: Script 1

'Hi (insert name),

My name is (your name) and I think I might be able to help you achieve (insert ROI). I work for (insert your company) and we work with similar companies including (insert customers). We offer (insert product/service), if it's something you're interested in learning more about I'd love to pop a bit more information across in an email.

If it's something you're open to, please just pop me your email address and I'll get some information sent across straight away'.

Audio message template: Script 2

'Hi *(insert name),*

I just wanted to send you a quick message because I loved your post on LinkedIn (insert post date). (Add some specific thoughts on the content.) I work in the industry as well, for a company called (your company). We actually work with companies like yours to help them achieve (insert ROI). We did some work recently with (insert customer) and helped them achieve (insert specific ROI). If you're interested, would it be ok to send you a little bit of information on it?'

Audio message template: Script 3

'Hi *(insert name),*

If I told you that I could help you achieve (insert ROI), would you be interested in learning more? If it's something you would be interested in, just let me know a good email address and I'll pop a little more information on how we might be able to do that for you'.

Audio message template: Script 4

'Hi (insert name),

I'm writing an article on LinkedIn with some top tips from experts in the (insert industry). I wanted to see if you might be able to spare a few minutes to share some of your tips? I'd love to include you in the article. If you're able to, let me know and I'll pop across the questions'.

OTHER LINKEDIN MESSAGING OPTIONS

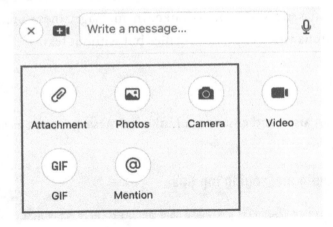

You are also able to send a few other forms of media via LinkedIn messages:

Images

You are able to send images via social media. This could be images of your product, or an image you think they might find valuable or entertaining.

Attachments

You can upload a document to a message, such as a proposal, leaflet, case study etc.

GIFs

You can send GIFs via a LinkedIn message; these are small humorous video clips, like memes but without text.

Emoji

You can also send emojis via LinkedIn messages such as smiley faces, etc.

LinkedIn messaging top tips

Hyper personalisation is key, make sure you DO YOUR HOMEWORK!

The more you make it about them and relevant to them, the better your chance of a reply.

Use messages to start conversations with prospects or people that can connect you to prospects.

If you think a pitch is the right approach, make sure it's focused on how THEY will benefit from working with you.

Test all three forms of messaging, written, audio and video to see which ones work best for you.

Treat everyone as an individual.

PART 5
CONTENT

'Content on LinkedIn is an untapped GOLDMINE of opportunity missed by 99% of salespeople'.

CHAPTER 14

SHARING CONTENT ON LINKEDIN

L et me show you just how much of an untapped goldmine LinkedIn content is ...

Out of all of the regular active LinkedIn users using it on a monthly basis, only 1% share content on a weekly basis. Yes, you read that right, *1%*! Of the 260 million LinkedIn members in 2019 who were using LinkedIn on a regular basis, only 1% of them were sharing content.

How insane is that?

Content (done right) generates inbound leads, generates outbound opportunities, grows your personal brand and can help you build and grow relationships.

What's even crazier than just 1% of LinkedIn users creating content is that MOST of the content being published on LinkedIn isn't any good! It's advertisement-focused content that not only offers very little value to the reader, but that also doesn't generate any engagement. I'll dig into this a bit more in the 80/20 section.

The best part though?

Once you understand how to do it right, it's not even that difficult.

In fact, you don't even have to spend a lot of time doing it.

Let me give you a quick example:

Not that long ago I wrote an article on LinkedIn. It took me approximately 30 minutes to write this particular article, which I then published on LinkedIn as soon as I had finished. Within 24 hours these were the results I achieved:

- 100,000+ Views
- 30,000+ Likes

- 3,000+ Comments
- 3,000+ Shares
- 15 Sales Enquiries
- 10 Won Bookings
- Value over £75,000 won revenue

Thirty minutes of time invested to generate those results, it's a pretty good ROI.

But Dan, I don't have hours every day to sit and create content! I'm too busy making calls, sending emails and sitting in meetings.

Most of the content that I will suggest that you share on a regular basis won't even take that long to create. In fact, I'd suggest not spending more than 5 to 10 minutes a day creating content on LinkedIn! I'm pretty sure that most of you reading this book will be able to find 5 to 10 minutes per day.

The best content on LinkedIn is authentic, value-giving content, and often quick and easy to create.

THINK BEFORE YOU SHARE

A lot of people who will be reading this book, which could include you, work for a company. You work for a brand and so I want to make a very important point. When you do anything on LinkedIn or social media that is FOR work, you need to remember that you REPRESENT work. When you post something, you're representing your company. When you send a message, you're representing your company.

As we work through all of the various ways you can create and share great content, it's always important to think before you share. Make sure that it aligns with your company brand, make sure it aligns with your personal brand and, more importantly, make sure it makes the RIGHT impression with your prospects and customers.

We are very used to using social media for personal reasons, not professional. Many of us use social media networks like Facebook, Instagram and others to post personal updates and personal opinions. When some people come to start using social media for professional reasons, they sometimes continue to use it in a personal way, sharing things that perhaps don't align well with the corporate brand, don't help them build a personal brand and don't make a good impression to potential prospects and customers.

Whilst I certainly don't want you to overthink everything you share, just make sure it is always professionally focused.

For example, posting a random picture of your kids on LinkedIn might not go down very well, but posting a picture of your kids with a message that's relevant will work better. Something like:

'Today my 8-year-old son made his very first sale ...

After spending half an hour painting a picture, he asked me whether I liked it.

Obviously, I loved it. I asked him if I could have it to put in my office.

He said sure, if you buy it!

How can I refuse that?

I asked him how much, he named a price, we negotiated, and he settled and closed the deal.

Ten minutes later, I returned to see what he was doing.

There were three more paintings already with another one in the works.

He asked me if when he finished, he could phone his Grandma, Grandad, Auntie, Uncle ...

He had more sales to make!'

That post, with a photo of my son and the painting, or a picture of me and my son holding the painting, becomes relevant. It's a message that aligns to my personal and corporate brand, as well as holds relevance and value to my audience, prospects and customers.

Before you share anything, just make sure it has the right intention and offers the right value to your audience.

THE MYSTERIOUS ALGORITHM ...

You may have heard people talking about the elusive LinkedIn 'algorithm'. Some people claim to know it, others express their curiosity about it. For anyone who doesn't know what this is, it's the process built into the social media network to sort out which posts its users see.

> Social media algorithms are a way of sorting posts in a user's feed based on relevancy instead of publish time. Social networks prioritise the content a user sees in their feed first by the likelihood that they'll actually want to see it.

Now here is the thing, it changes all of the time and no one knows (or at least very few people know) what it is. For social media companies this is their secret sauce, the variety of algorithms used defines their networks, so it's rarely something that is ever broadcast.

The LinkedIn algorithm …

Whilst you're very unlikely to see LinkedIn tell people what the algorithm is, there is a way to at least, on a basic level, have an understanding of it. In the world of content on LinkedIn, this can prove to be hugely beneficial.

I'll give you an example:

In 2018, LinkedIn programmed their algorithm to push organic videos uploaded onto it.

'But Dan, you just said that NO ONE knows what the algorithm is?'

That's true, and I have no direct proof that this was the case, but I have some evidence that heavily supports my conclusion.

Early in 2018 I started to test video content on my page The Daily Sales. Prior to this, I was sharing photo-based content and memes. At the time, the engagement was driving follower growth by around 800 new followers per month.

After sharing video content on The Daily Sales, within the first month follower growth rocketed to around 5,000 new followers. Engagement was through the roof; where a photo or meme would get around 300 likes, videos were pulling 3,000 likes. After the second month, follower growth surpassed 8,000 new followers per month.

Because I kept a close eye on the results, I continued to create and share video content (alongside normal content as well). I was able to ride this wave for nearly six months, during which time LinkedIn was pushing video content out further than other forms of content, and gained a huge growth in my audience, engagement with my content and business generated from it as well.

Whilst it's very rare for anyone to truly know what the LinkedIn algorithm is doing, keeping an eye out for forms of content performing above average can be a good way to get an idea of what it's doing.

CREATE VS CURATE

There are two core ways that you can share content on LinkedIn. The first is to share other people's content, you 'curate' it. You might find a really interesting article in the news or see someone share something that you think your audience will benefit from. Then there is 'creating' content where you create and publish your own content on LinkedIn.

Both are valuable, but creating your own content is a lot more valuable.

Here are some of the more common forms of content found on LinkedIn:

- Article/Blog
- Post/Update
- Image
- Video
- Quote
- PDF Document

There are two very important points I want to make around the types of content ...

The LinkedIn algorithm will push certain types of content, but it changes all of the time. When I first started using LinkedIn, the algorithm was pushing published articles. That was the best form of content on the platform. Fast forward to 2020 and it's currently long-form, text-based posts on LinkedIn that are favoured and generating the most engagement.

Unfortunately, LinkedIn doesn't reveal what the algorithm is pushing, and as I mentioned it changes consistently. The best way to learn what's working best is to listen to some of the experts out there who may know, and also just look at your feed. Which forms of content are performing best on a consistent basis?

A BALANCED LINKEDIN CONTENT DIET ...

Variety truly is key. One of the biggest traps I see people falling into on LinkedIn is just repeating the same form of content over and over.

I've seen it time and time again over the years. People start sharing content and it gets engagement. They keep doing it, and over a few weeks or months they build a strong personal brand and start to generate big numbers of engagement.

So, what do they do? They keep doing the same thing! I mean if it ain't broke, why fix it, right?

What happens after a little while is that their audience gets bored of seeing the same stories told in the same way, so the engagement drops. Next thing you know, instead of getting 100–200+ likes like they used to, they struggle to get 20. Variety really is key to combat this. Don't just share long-form, text posts; add in a video once a week or once a fortnight, add in a photo once a week, write a blog once a month.

That variety will not only help you carve out a long-term success strategy on LinkedIn, but it will also help you reach even more people. It's the exact same principle of the prospecting maze where different people have different preferences for communication. Some prefer to use the phone, some prefer to use social media, some prefer instant messages, etc.

Well, in the content world we also each have different content form preferences. Some people prefer long-form, text-based posts, some people prefer videos, some people prefer articles, and so on.

This is why variety is crucial, as it will help you carve out a long-term LinkedIn strategy and will also help you reach the maximum number of people and prospects.

'Eighty per cent of the content you share on LinkedIn should be VALUABLE to your prospects and customers'.

THE 80/20 RULE OF CONTENT ON LINKEDIN

In sales many of us will know the 80/20 rule, that 80% of your sales will come from 20% of your customers. I've found that rule to also be applicable to content on LinkedIn, just in a slightly different way. You see, most salespeople, in fact most companies using LinkedIn that share content, tend to share content that gives NO VALUE to their audience.

More often than not their content is all about them.

Here are our latest offers, look at our new case study, check out our latest blog about us, me, me, me, blah, blah, blah.

In reality the content offers very little, if no value at all, to their prospects and their audience. The content then fails to generate any engagement and so offers minimal value to the salesperson or business they represent.

This is where the problem lies ...

Eighty per cent of the content often shared by salespeople at the moment and by companies isn't valuable to the audience, it's only valuable to the company.

Then what you find is that 20% of the content that they share has value to the audience; every so often they might share a nice team photo, or something insightful.

What I would highly recommend is that you flip that right around.

Make it so that 80% of the content you share IS valuable to your audience. Whether that's entertaining, insightful, educational, motivational, as long as it genuinely offers value to the reader/viewer, then it's good.

What this does is earn you the opportunity to make around 20% of your content about you, your product and your offers. The big difference will be that because you've shared so much value to your audience before, you'll generate more engagement on your advertisement-style content. People will be more interested because you've given something to them first, rather than just asked for something from them.

As you work through this content chapter, always have in your mind that 80% of your content should be valuable to your audience. Then you'll have the opportunity to share and promote yourself afterwards.

HOW TO START SHARING CONTENT ON LINKEDIN

The easiest place to start with content is sharing other people's content. Oddly enough, the majority of salespeople who do use LinkedIn already do this. All they do, though, is re-share their company's content. So, marketing publishes a blog or article on LinkedIn or from their website, and then the sales team are told to share it.

One of the worst ways you can do this is to 'blind' share, which means simply clicking the share icon and sharing it directly to your feed. Blind sharing will very rarely generate any results or any form of engagement. There is simply minimal value to the audience and, unless it's a super-amazing article, this tactic is unlikely to encourage the audience to click on and read it.

When sharing external content, I'd highly recommend adding your thoughts to it. Even if it's just a few lines or sentences, it starts to add value to the share.

Quite possibly the BEST article ever on sales methodologies!

Fantastic dive into the top 10 methodologies with some amazing tips and insights into how you can find the best one for you.

There really is no "one size fits all" with sales methodologies, I've used several of these over the years and it really does differ to what you sell and who you sell to as to which one is best for you.

This article will definitely help! Let me know which sales methodologies you use or have used in the comments.....

Tell people why you enjoyed that post or article, what you enjoyed about it, what it made you think of, perhaps some questions it made you think of, anything that starts to give people an insight into your world and also encourages them to read the shared post/article as well.

FINDING CONTENT TO SHARE

There is a whole host of amazing content out there, but it's unfortunately hidden under an even bigger stack of bad content! Finding good content to share isn't always easy, but there are a few things you can do to help.

FOLLOW INDUSTRY INFLUENCERS – Find the best industry influencers on their social pages, whether that's LinkedIn, Facebook, Twitter, etc. They will often share great content on a daily basis that could be great to share to your audience. Make sure they're industry relevant and make a note to check them on a regular basis.

SUBSCRIBE TO NEWSLETTERS – This is one of the best ways you can make sharing content more efficient. Find all of the best industry news channels and newsletters out there and subscribe to their email newsletters. This allows you to then direct all of the latest news and content to your inbox on a regular basis. Over the years I have always made sure that I am subscribed to all of the best industry-relevant news channels and every day I read through all of the emails to find the best content to share.

ADD CONTENT PLATFORMS TO YOUR FAVOURITES –
Another great little 'hack' is to add the best content platforms and news channels to your favourites list on your web
browser. This just makes it that little bit easier to click into
them and go straight to the places that you know are likely
to have good content to share.

CHAPTER 15

CREATING CONTENT ON LINKEDIN

This is where the opportunity really lies, creating your own content.

Understandably this is also one of the areas that scares a lot of salespeople (and also the companies that they work for).

I mean, the thought of all of their salespeople writing their own content can be pretty scary! However, I need you to trust me and understand that the potential far outweighs the risk. The key is to do it right and understand how to avoid some of the risks.

I'd like to remind you that before using LinkedIn, I had never ever created a piece of content before, I didn't even really know what content was! I'd never written a blog, never recorded a video, never created a meme, none of it. I was just a traditional salesperson making calls. What I have done in this section of the book, and in my training courses, is make content creation as simple and easy as possible.

In this section I will talk you through each of the core content types, and how you can create the best possible content for each of them. I'll include some examples and top tips as well, along with some quick start ideas for you.

Case study – From LinkedIn article to closed sale

Very early on in my LinkedIn journey I started to write my own articles. I had been reading articles from some of the leading thought leaders around the world and felt inspired to try sharing my own stories and experiences in the world of sales.

At the time, I was selling into the IT industry and trying to connect with IT Directors and IT Managers to sell an industry-recognised training package. I'd been trying to reach the IT Director of a medium-sized technical support business for a few weeks but had no luck in getting through to them on the phone, email or even face to face.

One day, after a few weeks of trying, I published a new article on LinkedIn. A few hours after it was published, I looked at the engagement. Scrolling through the likes I noticed that one of the sales reps from the company I was trying to prospect had clicked like on my article.

A lightbulb lit in my mind …

Now, this wasn't the IT Director clicking like, it wasn't even someone in the IT department. However, someone within that company had enjoyed the article that I had written and shared.

Top tip

When you create and share content on LinkedIn, whether it's a blog, post, video, photo, etc., you can't see the people that 'View' the content. You could get 1,000 views, but you'll never be able to see who they are.

When they engage with the content, such as clicking 'like', commenting or sharing the content, THAT'S when you can actually see them.

Once you can see them, you can connect with them and use it to start a conversation with them. This is why I encourage everyone creating content on LinkedIn with the goal of generating sales and clients to drive as much engagement to their content as possible.

It's only through the engagement that you can actually see who is engaging and start talking to them.

After realising that this sales rep had clicked like, I knew I had an opportunity to find a different route to my target decision-maker.

I connected with the sales rep and sent them a nice simple conversational message (which you'll have seen earlier in the book):

Hi John,

Thank you for clicking like on my article! I hope you enjoyed it; I'd love to know what your thoughts were on the subject?

Kind Regards,

Dan

They replied straightaway, and we started chatting. I didn't jump in trying to pitch them, neither did I jump in and immediately ask for the phone number of their IT Director. Instead, I talked to them about the subject of the article which they liked.

We sent a few messages back and forth, building a nice little bit of rapport, where I had then earned the opportunity to discuss what I was selling.

That's when I mentioned that I had been trying to reach their IT Director to discuss what I was selling. They were more than happy to make an introduction and actually went on to arrange a phone call for me with them.

After that phone call, I was able to progress to a meeting and eventually go on to win that sale.

HASHTAGS AND TAGS

Before I go through all of the different forms of content, I want to touch on hashtags and tagging people.

Let me first share a few important truths about hashtags and tagging people on LinkedIn …

THEY'RE NOT A SHORTCUT OR 'HACK' TO QUICK ENGAGEMENT!

One of the biggest mistakes I unfortunately see so many people making is they write 10+ hashtags on each post and then tag the same 10+ people in each post. They do this to try and generate more engagement, which on some occasions works. The problem is they end up getting the same engagement, from the same people, who are often friends or colleagues and not prospects or customers.

These posts look desperate and show the person to be only interested in generating a number, not providing any real value. It's like when a salesperson only talks about features and benefits, and not the actual problem that the prospect may have.

They are important, though ...

I want to be super-clear here, hashtags and tagging people are super-important when it comes to sharing and creating content on LinkedIn. However, it is also important that you use them in the right way.

HASHTAGS

Hashtags help make your content more visible. Right now, on LinkedIn a lot of people follow their favourite hashtags or the hashtags for their relevant industry. This helps them find the most relevant content when they want it.

When sharing or creating your own content, I'd recommend having no more than two or three hashtags per post. Find the most popular hashtags likely to be used by your prospects and customers and hopefully ones that are the most popular in your industry. For example, I tend to use #socialselling #sales #LinkedIn.

TAGGING PEOPLE

When you're writing a post on LinkedIn, if you press the @ symbol, a list of names should appear next to it. As you then start to type a person's name, the list should eventually find that person and once you click on their name, they will be tagged in the post.

The benefit of this is that they will receive a notification informing them that they have been tagged in your post. This often has a roll-on effect of encouraging those tagged in the post to engage with it quite quickly, which can really help drive the engagement of the post.

Similar to hashtags, I would recommend tagging two or three people in a post, but only when it is relevant and makes sense. You do not need to, and should not, tag people in every post that you share. For example, if you were attending an industry event and you were writing a summary of the day, you could tag in the speakers that you enjoyed listening to, perhaps some of the people you met or spoke to as well.

You can tag more than two or three people, but only when you need to. For the event example above, you could tag lots of people as you're likely to have seen lots of people and it makes sense. If you were just sharing a motivational quote, it perhaps wouldn't make sense to tag anyone in it, apart from perhaps the person who introduced you to that quote or the author of the quote.

POST/UPDATE

Character Limit – 1,300

A post or update is simply a written post on LinkedIn. There are two forms of post/update:

Short form – Typically one or two lines to one or two para-graphs max, these are short simple posts.
Long form – These use nearly all of the character limit and tell more of a story.

Both short- and long-form work really well on LinkedIn. What I have found, however, is that short-form tends to only work after you've built a strong personal brand. It's hard to get engagement with a short-form post when you haven't established a strong personal brand or built a strong network on LinkedIn.

I'd recommend starting with long-form LinkedIn posts, and then as your personal brand starts to build you can drip-feed short-form posts into it as well.

Right now, in 2020, long-form posts are quite possibly the best form of content on LinkedIn. They are the ones generating the most engagement and have one of the biggest impacts on your personal brand. The LinkedIn algorithm currently seems to favour them, as do a lot of people using LinkedIn.

THE FIRST THREE LINES ...

When you write a post/update on LinkedIn, only the FIRST THREE LINES will be visible (210 characters) to those who see it in their feed. They will then have to click on the post to open it up and read the rest. Whether you do a short-form or long-form post, you need to make sure those first three lines are super-engaging.

Otherwise people won't click to read the whole thing and won't engage with it!

The first three lines are like the bait you attach to a fishing hook ...

They will ultimately determine whether or not your post gets read and whether or not it generates any engagement. I've seen some amazing posts in terms of the value given or the story told, but the way they were written, and the first three lines were so bad that they didn't generate any engagement.

Make the start of the post exciting, then expand on the topic and close the post in an exciting way.

Case study – A post a day to LinkedIn fame

A couple of years ago I saw a sales trainer, with zero brand on LinkedIn, start to post on a daily basis.

They would write a long-form post every day, Monday through Friday, at 08:00. At first their posts would get a few likes, but nothing amazing. However, as each week passed, the engagement grew.

After a few months, their posts were getting hundreds of likes, with a few posts starting to do viral numbers as well. They jumped from a few hundred connections on LinkedIn to nearly 20,000 in the space of months. Their personal brand became globally known, and all they would do is write a new post every single day on LinkedIn, at the same time of 08:00.

The secret to their success wasn't posting at 08:00, though (before you start scheduling a post for 08:00 tomorrow!). The secret was in the value ...

Each and every single one of their posts offered value to their audience and to the industry which they were selling into. They were a mixture of educational, insightful, entertaining and thought provoking. None of their posts advertised anything or promoted anything.

Just one single post per day, at the same time, valuable to their audience, consistently.

Post examples

Daniel Disney
Keynote Speaker - Social Selling & LinkedIn Trainer -
Founder and Owner of The Daily Sales
1mo

Trick or treating is like cold calling training for kids...

#sales #coldcalling #halloween

153   16 Comments • 11,501 Views

👍 Like   💬 Comment   ➡ Share

📈 **11,501 views** of your post

Daniel Disney
International Keynote & Sales Kickoff Speaker | Author | LinkedIn & Social Se...
3mo • 🌐

Most salespeople aren't bad
Most salespeople don't pressure customers
Most salespeople don't sell ice to Eskimos
Most salespeople don't lie
Most salespeople don't send spammy messages
Most salespeople aren't deceptive
Most salespeople aren't selfish
Most salespeople aren't greedy
Most salespeople aren't scary

Most salespeople don't live up to the stereotype that most customers are scared
of

Most salespeople are good

Most salespeople want to help people

Most salespeople work their butts off to serve their customers

Don't judge the many on the few

The salesperson that you ghost or ignore or turn away might just be a salesperson
trying to help you

- They're probably trying to save you money
- They're probably trying to help your business grow
- They're probably trying to help you achieve a good ROI

Just because they have sales in their title or work in a sales role doesn't make them a bad salesperson

Most are good, hard working honest professionals doing their best to help

Judge them quickly and you may miss out

If you're a good salesperson click "like" on this post and let's show the world just how many there are

#sales #professionalselling #leadership

  2,741 · 278 Comments

 Like   Comment   ➔ Share   ◁ Send

 165,026 views of your post in the feed

Daniel Disney   • • •
International Keynote & Sales Kickoff Speaker | Author | LinkedIn & Social Se...
8mo · 🌐

I spoke to 2 Sales Managers recently and the conversations scared me quite a bit...

The first one asked whether they could install cameras into their sales reps HOMES to watch them and make sure they were working

The second one said there was no way they could EVER trust their sales team to work from home so they were still making them come to the office

These are some really scary comments that highlight some real leadership issues

If you can't trust your sales team you need to start looking at one thing...

A MIRROR!

The problem isn't them, it's you

YOU hired them
YOU trained them
YOU chose the systems
YOU manage them

If you can't trust them, YOU need to change

Right now a lot of companies don't have a choice, your sales teams HAVE to work from home

If you didn't trust them before you're going to have to start trusting them now

That doesn't mean sit at home and HOPE they make calls

It means actually LEADING them

- Set clear (realistic) goals
- Provide support
- Give them the tools they need
- Coach them

Salespeople right now are CRUSHING it working at home, it can be done

It's on you leaders out there to help them succeed right now

Now is when REAL leaders will stand out

Now is when REAL leaders (and their teams) will succeed

#leadership #sales #salestips

👍 💬 ❤️ 1,131 · 206 Comments

👍 Like   💬 Comment   ↪ Share   ✈ Send

📊 **96,750** views of your post in the feed

LinkedIn post/update ideas

- Share a story of how you overcame an obstacle or challenge in work.
- Share a lesson that you learned from a good manager that you had.
- Share a lesson that you learned from a bad manager that you've had.
- Share your top tips for your prospects right now.
- Share your personal favourite five to 10 professional books.

IMAGES/PHOTOS

Social media networks thrive on photos and images. LinkedIn, Facebook, Twitter, Instagram, they are filled with images daily and they generate amazing engagement. Images come in a whole variety of forms, and on LinkedIn you will find things like:

– Selfies
– Team photos
– Desk photos

- Photos of books
- Celebration photos
- Travel photos

The key benefit of sharing photos is it allows people to see into your world, and this is what social media is all about. This is why people are glued to their feed, they're interested in what everyone is doing. In the B2B professional world, it's not much different to the personal world.

From a sales perspective I see it like this ...

We all know that people buy from people they know, like and trust. There are few better ways of showing people who you are and getting them to know, like and trust you than from sharing on social media. Images help you achieve that.

Share photos of you in the office, photos of you with your colleagues or customers, photos of you at events. The more people see you, the more they'll get to know you. The more they get to know you, the bigger your personal brand will grow.

An extra opportunity ...

One of the great ways you can leverage LinkedIn to grow your personal brand and sell is to share stories about you personally, and not just professionally. Again, this needs to be done as part of a balanced variety of content, and you need to make sure it hits the right tone, but it's a great opportunity to really let people get to know you and build trust with them.

For example:

Not long ago I shared a photo on LinkedIn. The photo was of me and my youngest son, Joshua, driving a little boat around on some water. A photo like that could be deemed not suitable for LinkedIn, but there was a message attached to it.

I didn't get to see my kids much this week....

After delivering 5 full days training back to back and followed by workin ...see more

Alongside the photo, I wrote a long-form text-based post, with a story that I knew was valuable to my audience and would connect with my connections, customers and prospects. You see, the week prior to that weekend had seen me work 16+ hour days each and every day, Monday to Friday. I had been delivering training every day that week and then in the evenings was fully booked on consultancy work and project work.

After not seeing my kids at all that week, I dedicated the weekend to them. That photo captured a day out near the sea where I took them shopping, we had food out and enjoyed some of the fun activities including driving these fun little boats (which, for the record, I was terrible at!).

Alongside this photo I explained how much I had been working that week and how that meant I didn't get to see my children. I explained that a lot of people on the road to success struggle to maintain the balance of work, life, family, friends, etc. And whilst that week I had let the scales tip heavily around work, I made sure that my kids had my full attention all weekend.

The post achieved a few things:

Firstly, it showed my network, customers and prospects that I work hard and am not afraid to put in the graft. Secondly, it showed them that I was busy and in-demand, all powerful impressions to make with customers and potential prospects.

Thirdly, and more importantly, people got to see me as a human being.

I said it before, people buy from people. People don't buy from salespeople who are just trying to sell something, they buy from people they trust. In this post and in this image I showed them that I wasn't just a salesperson, or a trainer, or a speaker, but that I was a father.

The post allowed people to see me as a human being, a hard-working human being who works for his kids. In a day where most prospects out there see salespeople as untrustworthy aggressive people, this is a powerful way to change that impression.

PHOTO EXAMPLES

I am going to share a few examples of how you can use photos and images to create engaging forms of content on LinkedIn.

EXAMPLE 1 – THE ORANGE TWIRL

I had dinner with a good friend of mine, Niraj Kapur (author of the bestselling sales books *Everybody Works in Sales* and *The Easy Sales Guide For Business Owners*). Whilst having dinner, I mentioned that I had seen on social media a limited-release chocolate bar flavour, the Orange Twirl. As someone who enjoys orange-flavoured chocolate I was excited to try this, but I could not find a bar in any shop near me! I must have checked in nearly 50 shops trying to find them.

After that meal, Niraj went away and made it his mission to find one, searching all the shops in his area. After two weeks he actually found some! Niraj then posted the chocolate bar with a lovely little note to me. This inspired me to turn this into a post around sales ...

Daniel Disney
Keynote Speaker - Social Selling & LinkedIn Trainer - Founder and Owner of The Daily Sales
2w

Little details can go a long way in sales...

Around 2 weeks ago I met with a good friend of ...see more

189   50 Comments · 14,274 Views

Salespeople have the opportunity to do things like this all of the time, but most don't. Now whilst Niraj isn't trying to sell me anything, if he WAS, that would have been such an amazing thing to do. Imagine if I was Niraj's prospect, and during a conversation he had listened to my excitement around this particular chocolate bar. For him to then go and make a real effort to find one and post it to me would make a HUGE impression!

In the highly competitive world of selling THIS is how you stand out.

So, this was how I presented this story on LinkedIn, using it as an example of what salespeople could do to make a bigger impact with their prospects. I turned a simple gift from a friend into a powerful, relevant post for the industry that I sell to. A post that connects with my audience and my prospects. By taking a photo of the chocolate bar and the business card I was able to bring the post to life, helping drive better engagement from it.

EXAMPLE 2 – A BOOK REVIEW

Sharing a review of a book you have read or are reading is a great form of content and something I've done on countless occasions over the years (if you've seen the bookshelf in my videos, you'll see I am quite fond of a good sales book!).

Writing about books that you have enjoyed or are enjoying works well because there will be people in your audience (potentially even prospects and customers) who have read the same book and also loved it, or who might be interested in reading that book after you recommend it, and so receiving great value from your post and recommendation.

If possible, I'd recommend taking a selfie of you holding the book that you are writing about, as this then allows your network to see you (which is hugely powerful for personal brand building). I will admit, though, it's quite tricky taking a selfie whilst holding a book! If you can't or don't want to, then try to take a good picture of the book on a table with good lighting. Some people also prop a business card or catalogue or something branded next to it for a bit of sneaky advertisement.

Then write a post with the picture talking about what you enjoyed about it, what you took away from it, why you would recommend it, etc.

You also have the opportunity to tag in the author, often then resulting in the author liking and commenting on the photo (meaning THEIR audience will see the post, driving extra engagement).

EXAMPLE 3 – THE EVENT PHOTO

A lot of salespeople will attend key industry events, expos or networking events to prospect for opportunities. These offer a perfect opportunity to take photos and share them on LinkedIn. Not only can you take good photos with people you meet and people you watch speak, but it shows that you are truly immersed in your industry and at the front line of it.

There are a few options here; if you have one really good photo, then you can share that. However, if you end up taking lots of photos, you can share multiple photos in one post, or you can collage multiple photos into one image and share that.

One of the best photo opportunities you can get at an event is if you're able to speak. This is a great way to show that you are not just immersed in your industry but you're a leader within your industry. Getting speaker slots isn't difficult if you can provide value to the event.

Daniel Disney • • •
Keynote Speaker - Social Selling & LinkedIn Trainer - Founder and Owner of The Daily Sales
2w

You can't beat a good audience selfie!

I had the most amazing time speaking at the   ...see more

😊👏❤ 114   11 Comments • 10,110 Views

If you are able to get the opportunity to speak, then I would highly recommend taking as many good photos as you can. Try to have someone taking photos of you on stage and, like the example above, take a good on-stage selfie whilst you are there as well.

Photo post ideas

- Take a selfie holding a professional work-relevant book that you're reading or have read and share a review of it (don't forget to tag the author).
- Take a photo of your work environment, either your home working environment or desk at work, and write a post about it.
- Take a photo with one of your colleagues or your manager and write about them.
- Take a screenshot of a team meeting or virtual team meeting and talk about your colleagues.

NOTE – THE 'LINKEDIN POLICE'

Now seems like an appropriate time to mention the LinkedIn police ...

I'll always chuckle to myself when I discuss this as I have a flashback to one of my LinkedIn Masterclasses. When I mentioned the 'LinkedIn Police', one attendee literally thought LinkedIn had its own police department to monitor content ☺.

Worry not, there is no LinkedIn police department; instead it is a self-imposed title given to those who feel they have the authority to say whether a piece of content is 'suitable' or 'appropriate' for LinkedIn (ultimately based on their own assumptions of what the social network should be).

When we look at sharing images on LinkedIn, it can be easy to get flagged by the LinkedIn police. Some people may comment on your photo that it isn't suitable for LinkedIn. My rule of thumb for this is to try and make sure it has relevance and value to your LinkedIn professional audience.

Some of the time, these 'LinkedIn Police' are just online trolls who are incorrect in their judgement of what is and isn't suitable for LinkedIn. Let's be fair and open-minded, though, sometimes content that is shared perhaps isn't suitable. I wouldn't want everyone thinking that ALL negative comments are trolling; sometimes there is good reason in them. However, a lot of the time, in my experience, when people say a post isn't suitable for LinkedIn, it often is perfectly fine.

QUOTES

Quotes are by far one of the most popular forms of content. They have been for many years now and continue to compete with good long-form updates and video. The best quotes are often motivational and inspirational quotes, although humorous quotes and statistic-based quotes also perform very well. On The Daily Sales, a lot of the quotes that I share do 2X, 3X and sometimes even up to 5X the engagement on LinkedIn of memes and articles that are shared.

I'd personally recommend that you turn the quote or statistic into an image, and then either share it on its own or with a post written with it. Something like this:

These do work very well on their own without any post written, but also work well when you write about what the quote means to you or perhaps if you share a story alongside it. The key is to use variety. Share some quotes on their own, and share some with a post.

The internet is FULL of motivational and inspirational quotes, and you can create image versions very easily. I use www.canva .com to create mine, but there are apps you can download on your phone to create them and tons of software tools available, some free and some paid, to create them.

MEMES

Anyone who follows The Daily Sales or has followed me for a while will know I'm fond of a good meme! Well, all right, I love memes! The Daily Sales' enormous and fast growth was heavily down to sharing a sales meme every single day. Memes and humour-based content also contributed massively to my own personal brand growth.

> WORD OF WARNING – Most memes use images that come from films and TV shows, which are often copyright protected. It is important to check with your manager or marketing department on whether the image is suitable and safe to use, and the tone/message of the meme aligns with the company brand.

For anyone who doesn't know what a meme is (and no judgement if you don't!), it's simply an image taken from something popular like a film or TV series from a particular scene or moment, with some words added to it that makes it relevant to other people.

For example:

Meme credit to Django Unchained (2012) Columbia Pictures. Credit to Yasmin Disney for adding the photo of my book to the meme image.

Memes are entertaining! In a LinkedIn world where so much of the content is serious, light and entertaining content like this often proves to be very popular. They show a sense of humour, which can be a hugely powerful tool in sales. Humour breaks down trust barriers and helps connect you with your prospects and customers in a much more human way.

I create all of my memes on a free meme creator app (Mematic), although there are plenty of alternative apps and websites where you can create perfect memes for free. Find a good or funny image and then think about an industry-relevant situation that it could relate to. Think of things that will be funny for your prospects and customers, as they are the people that you want to engage with.

Similar to quotes, these images can be shared on their own or with a written post. I would recommend doing both: sometimes share the meme on its own, and sometimes share it with some thoughts as well.

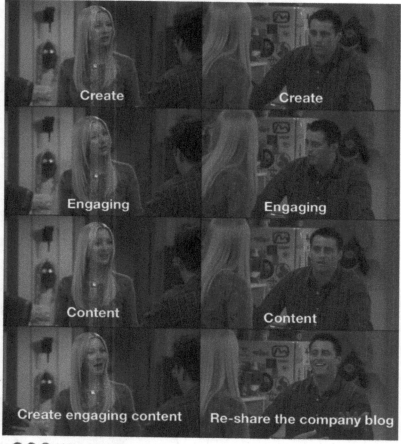

1,032 · 109 Comments

Memes credit Friends TV series.

PDF

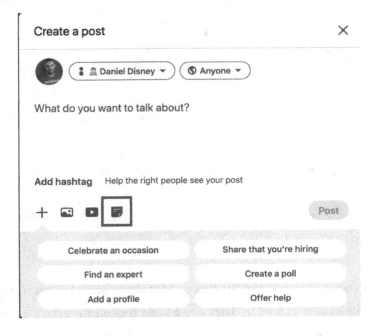

You can also upload a PDF document as a form of media on LinkedIn. For example, if you're looking for a job, you could upload a copy of your CV for potential recruiters or employers to view.

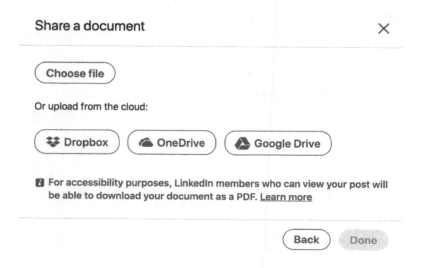

You could create a top 10 tips guide, share each tip on a page and upload it as a PDF. They are a little more interactive as you need to scroll across to read through each one.

For anyone who hasn't created a PDF before, you can write/create the content on Microsoft Word or PowerPoint, and then save it as a PDF when you save the file. This will convert it into PDF form which you can then share on LinkedIn.

One of the PDF posts I did recently was sharing '10 Ways to Generate Leads with Social Selling'. There were 12 slides/pages in total (the opening page, the 10 tips, one per page) and then a closing page which had my website, a photo of me and a picture of my book to drive people to learn more.

Daniel Disney
International Keynote & Sales Kickoff Speaker | Author | LinkedIn & Social Se...
6mo • 🌐

Here's the secret to building a HUGE personal brand on LinkedIn...

It takes just 3 simple steps   ...see more

3 Steps To Building A HUGE Personal Brand on LinkedIn • 11 pages

1 / 11 ●

👍 👏 ❤️ 154 · 61 Comments

LINKEDIN POLLS

LinkedIn polls are an amazing form of content that give you the chance to gain and share unique and valuable insights from your network. Not only that, but they also give you some brilliant sales and lead generating opportunities.

They work by giving you the chance to ask your LinkedIn audience (and anyone else outside of your audience who sees the post) a question. You're able to give them up to four possible answers to vote for.

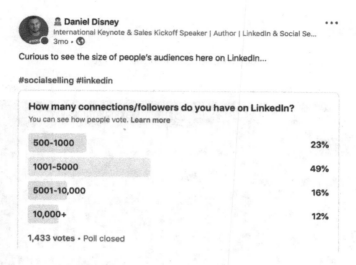

Daniel Disney
International Keynote & Sales Kickoff Speaker | Author | LinkedIn & Social Se...
3mo ·

Curious to see the size of people's audiences here on LinkedIn...

#socialselling #linkedin

How many connections/followers do you have on LinkedIn?
You can see how people vote. Learn more

500-1000	23%
1001-5000	49%
5001-10,000	16%
10,000+	12%

1,433 votes · Poll closed

LinkedIn has been clever with these as when you see them appear on your LinkedIn newsfeed, the only way that you can see the results is to vote yourself! Which helps drive engagement to them.

Where they go wrong ...

Unfortunately, like with all forms of content, a lot of people get these wrong. The key is to ask the right questions. When you ask the wrong questions, you can end up with minimal (or sometimes zero) votes.

TOP TIP – Try to ask questions that are relevant and valuable to your audience right now. You want people to either have a strong opinion on the subject enough to vote on it or be interested enough in the answers to want to see the results.

Create a post   ✕

👤 👤 Daniel Disney ▾   🌐 Anyone ▾

What do you want to talk about?

Add hashtag   Help the right people see your post

➕ 🖼️ ▶️ 🗒️   Post

Celebrate an occasion	Share that you're hiring
Find an expert	Create a poll
Add a profile	Offer help

Create a poll   ✕

Your question *

E.g., How do you commute to work?

0/140

Option 1 *

E.g., Public transportation

0/30

Option 2 *

E.g., Drive myself

0/30

(+ Add option)

Poll duration

1 week   ▾

We don't allow requests for political opinions, medical information or other
sensitive data.

(Back)   Done

TURNING POLLS INTO SALES

There are a few ways you can leverage polls to generate leads and sales. Firstly, by creating engaging industry-relevant polls, alongside a consistent strong personal brand, you can generate inbound enquiries. I've personally generated some great inbound leads from people that I've been connected with for a period of time, who have seen my content and found the poll valuable and insightful. The poll was what tipped the scales and encouraged them to message me regarding an opportunity to work with them.

From an outbound lead generation perspective, you then have a couple of great opportunities. Firstly, the same as all other forms of content, you have the engagement. People clicking like, people sharing and people writing comments. Any of those who pre-qualify as a prospect should be messaged. Here is an example template:

'Hi Sarah,

Thank you for your comment on my LinkedIn poll today! I'm glad you liked the subject, did you vote?

It's been interesting looking at the results!

Kind regards

Dan'

(Remember, the key is to start a CONVERSATION, not pitch your product!)

The other opportunity you have to generate sales is from the people who actually vote. LinkedIn allows you to see everyone who votes. You can scroll through those votes, pre-qualify your prospects and then use that to start a conversation.

For any of this to work, the polls need to be valuable and engaging. Unfortunately, a poor, non-engaging post isn't going to be a good setup for lead generation! Here are some ideas on poll subjects that might help you create some engaging (and lead generating) LinkedIn polls:

LinkedIn poll ideas

1. **How long have you worked in (insert industry)?**
   Less than one year, one to three years, three to five years, five to 10+ years
2. **Do you read any of these leading industry blogs/news sites?**
   Insert selection of blogs/news sites
3. **What percentage of your team works remotely?**
   Less than 10%, 10–25%, 25–50%, 50–100%
4. **How many business books do you read each month?**
   1–3, 3–5, 5–10, None

VIDEO POSTS ON LINKEDIN

Video is one of the most powerful forms of content out there.

Think about it, when you write something people can read your words. When you record something, they hear your voice. When you share a video, they get to see you. It's the closest media form to being face-to-face, which in the world of sales is king.

We consume video in huge amounts, YouTube has become THE video platform, but people share videos across all social media sites, Facebook, Twitter, Instagram, TikTok and so on.

Video content on LinkedIn, similar to other forms of content, is done brilliantly by some and terribly by others. Before I share some of the common mistakes made by people when sharing or creating videos, I want to share a quick example of a few mistakes made by one individual sales rep on LinkedIn:

AN EXAMPLE OF HOW *NOT* TO RECORD A VIDEO FOR LINKEDIN ...

A sales rep who is in my network on LinkedIn shared their first video and it came up in my feed. Now, I'm genuinely excited when I see sales reps start to share videos on LinkedIn. I know how scary it can be recording and sharing your first video (almost as scary as making your first cold call!).

The video was them simply sharing some updates on their company. However, there were a few problems.

Firstly, they chose quite possibly the worst place in their office to record the video. They were standing in a corner in their office, with one extremely dirty wall with paint peeling off it on one side. The other side was a window, which again was VERY dirty and showed a very miserable British grey day outside.

The next problem was their shirt, oh, their shirt ...

They were wearing a white shirt which had the BIGGEST coffee stain down the front from the collar to below the video screen!

This, mixed with a general scruffy appearance and very stutter-filled delivery, made for a very low-quality video.

Let us not forget that this rep represents their company, they represent their brand, they represent their product.

Their customers will see that video, their prospects will see that video and their industry will see that product.

Unfortunately, these are common mistakes I see people make on LinkedIn when sharing videos. Again, don't get me wrong, I know it's not easy building the confidence to share video.

However, it is so important that you think before you post, and you pay attention to the details. The video you share could be the FIRST impression that you make with a prospect or could be seen by your valuable customers.

REMEMBER THE VIDEO MESSAGING TIPS …

In the messaging section we explored some of the important aspects of videos that you need to think about. You will see a lot of similarity with video content; most of the principles and key factors are the same. We will just explore them in more detail here as there is a bigger variety of video content forms compared to video messages.

Here are some of the common mistakes that people make when creating and sharing videos on LinkedIn:

- Recording with a poor choice of background
- Not dressed appropriately for their role/company
- No branding in the background or on the video
- No subtitles/captions in the video

DO YOU NEED TO HAVE SUBTITLES/CAPTIONS?

It has been said that up to 80% of videos watched on social media are watched on MUTE. That's right, the majority of video content is consumed with no sound, yet most of the videos on LinkedIn DON'T have subtitles or captions. (The main reason that many don't have the volume up on LinkedIn is that a large percentage are utilising it at work.)

I've tested posting videos with and without captions and in my personal experience captions make a very big difference to the engagement that video generates. This has also been supported by other LinkedIn video creators from around the world.

There are plenty of ways that you can add subtitles/captions; after reviewing many I use a platform called Zubtitle.

It's incredibly easy to use, you simply record the video and upload it to Zubtitle. Their software then creates the captions, often in minutes. You can review them and make any edits. (I'd highly recommend doing this as it can sometimes misinterpret what you're saying.) Once you're happy you simply download the video with the captions added.

170 · 40 Comments · 3,779 Views

LINKEDIN LIVE

Prerecording and sharing videos is one of the best forms of content; however, hosting LIVE videos takes it to the next level.

You can deliver live, interactive videos to your audience, including your prospects. Live videos have already proven to be hugely popular forms of content on other social media networks such as Facebook and Instagram and they've become very popular on LinkedIn as well.

One of the many benefits to LIVE videos on LinkedIn is that it notifies people in your network when you're live, which helps encourage more people to watch, instead of only showing it on the feed.

Daniel Disney
International Keynote & Sales Kickoff Speaker | Author | LinkedIn & Social Se...
2w · 🌐

Ask me anything today and I'll also be sharing some of my top tips for closing more opportunities before the end of the month and building more pipeline in November!

At the time of writing this book early in 2021, LinkedIn LIVE is only available through an application and approval process. Many LinkedIn users are applying every day, and many are not getting approved. Some people get approved after applying three or four times, some after six to eight+ times (it took me six application attempts before I was approved).

Here is the link to start the application process and learn more about how it works –

https://business.linkedin.com/marketing-solutions/linkedin-live/getting-started

Not only do you have to apply to stream LIVE videos on LinkedIn, but you can't stream directly through LinkedIn. Unlike Facebook, where you stream through the social network site, LinkedIn requires you to stream through a third-party platform.

They do provide you with a list of recommended platforms; the one I use is called StreamYard. They have a free version and some paid versions as well. Once you're approved on LinkedIn, you'll be sent a link to instructions for setting it up, which will include choosing and setting up one of these platforms.

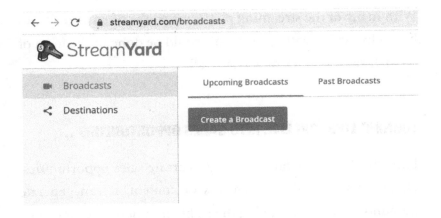

To go live on LinkedIn, you will do it through the third-party platform. For example, I log into StreamYard and click the 'create broadcast' button. This then asks me which sites I want to stream on (you can stream to multiple social media sites at the same time). On StreamYard you have the opportunity to customise your screen, so if you look at the image at the start of this section, you'll see I have a banner around the edges of the video which I created at www.canva.com and uploaded. There are then lot of different things you can customise, such as having names or different text at the bottom.

When you are live, on StreamYard you are able to see the comments on the right-hand side. Whilst unfortunately you can't reply to the comments through the streaming site, you're able to read them and reply verbally through the video.

With many of the streaming platforms you're often also able to host a live video with guests. This could be done in the form of an interview, a panel, or a group talk.

TURNING LINKEDIN LIVE INTO SALES OPPORTUNITIES ...

LinkedIn LIVE is a fantastic way to create sales opportunities. Done right, like all other forms of content, it can generate inbound enquiries by giving the right amount of relevant value to your prospects. This is always enhanced if it is supported by the consistent building of a strong personal brand.

Like other forms of content, you have the opportunity to generate outbound leads by leveraging the engagement of the video. You can look at who clicks like, who comments and who shares the live video to then qualify and message those who fit your prospect criteria.

Another opportunity that you could use to generate sales opportunities from a LinkedIn LIVE is to interview your prospect, or someone from within your prospective company. They get the benefit of the exposure and the value of being seen as someone credible in the industry while you get the benefit of getting to speak to them, learn about them and start building a relationship with them.

This is the same principle as the 'Industry Expert Blog' message template and very similar to the process used by a lot of podcast hosts out there. They create a mutually beneficial situation where the prospect gets immense value from being a guest in the blog/podcast/live video and you create a much nicer, warmer introduction to them compared to a cold call.

THE KEY, AS ALWAYS, IS TO DO THIS WITH AUTHENTICITY

It's okay to invite a prospect onto your LinkedIn LIVE if it genuinely has value to them. This isn't something that you can spam out there. If you do this without being authentic or without it offering value to them, you'll struggle to generate a result.

NOTE – It's worth mentioning to not make assumptions when thinking about the value to them. Some of you might read this and think, 'Well, it's okay for you, Daniel, you have a big audience and brand on LinkedIn so the value to them is obvious'.

Look, you may only have 500 connections or followers on LinkedIn, but that's probably 500 connections/followers that they DON'T have. That's 500 people that THEIR company will now be in front of. That could help THEM generate customers, it creates content that THEY can use.

LinkedIn LIVE Ideas:

- Host LIVE videos where you share stories, insights, tips or ideas.
- Host a LIVE interview with an industry expert.
- Host a LIVE interview with someone very experienced in the industry.
- Host a LIVE interview with an industry author.
- Host a LIVE panel with several key industry experts or relevant people.
- Host a LIVE interview with an industry expert from WITHIN your company.
- Host LIVE videos where you review industry-relevant books or business books.
- Host a LIVE panel with a group of your colleagues sharing industry stories.

EXTRA THOUGHTS/TIPS

Many platforms will record the stream, which you can then use in little clips for future content and upload onto YouTube as well.

You can also turn the content from the video into a blog/article or even an eBook to share.

Promote your LIVE video in advance by creating an event on LinkedIn and inviting people to join.

LINKEDIN STORIES

Stories are bite-size mini-forms of content allowing users to give snapshot insights into their days and provide super-engaging updates. They consist of either images or short videos that last for 24 hours on LinkedIn. You can only post stories from the LinkedIn mobile app and these can be shared on personal profiles and company pages.

Personal profiles – Using LinkedIn stories through your personal profile is a great way to grow your personal brand even further and give people an insight into your daily activities. For example, you can share insights into places you're visiting, people you're speaking to, meetings that you're having, prospects/customers that you're meeting, events that you're attending, etc.

Company pages – Using LinkedIn stories through your company page is a great way to let people see the people behind the corporate brand. You can share insights into the office, team meetings, insights into individual team members, leaders, etc.

CHAPTER 16

WRITING ARTICLES ON LINKEDIN

Articles or blogs on LinkedIn are one of the most effective forms of content out there, especially for generating a strong ROI.

The benefit of an article over other forms of content on LinkedIn is you give significantly more value and content within it, earning you the opportunity to talk about yourself and what you do at the end.

You don't have the opportunity to do this in a text post, an image post, a video, or a poll.

This is why the ROI is often higher for articles. You'll see in the examples that I share in this chapter how an article gives a much greater value, which then leads to a call to action and about me section, which helps drive more inbound leads.

As with all forms of content, the key is in the quality. The key to writing a successful article on LinkedIn is made up of several components which I'll walk you through in this chapter.

Case study – Blog to closed deal in 24 Hours

Early in 2019 I wrote and published an article on LinkedIn. It proved to be an extremely popular article, and within hours it had thousands of views and plenty of likes, comments and shares. The article had taken me about an hour to write, which was slightly longer than I would usually spend writing an article, but I had a bit more to write in this one.

Four hours after publishing the article, a message pinged into my LinkedIn inbox.

It was a lead from someone interested in booking me to be the keynote speaker at their big annual conference later that year. The message read:

Hi Dan,

I really enjoyed the article you shared today. We have our annual conference coming up later this year and I was interested to see whether you might be available/interested in being our keynote speaker. We would love you to talk on the subject you discuss in your article.

Kind Regards,

Prospect

I replied straightaway, thanking them for their kind words about my article and expressing an interest in speaking at their event. I gave them my email address and asked if they could kindly send me some more information about the event, dates, location, etc. Within 30 minutes an email came through that provided more details on the opportunity.

After that I was able to put together a quote and some ideas on what could make the keynote as good as possible. A couple of hours later an email came back confirming that they wanted to book me and requesting my speaker contract and agreement to be sent across. After putting that together and sending it across it was then approximately 30 minutes before I had the signed contract and agreement sent back.

Less than 24 hours after publishing the article on LinkedIn I had generated and closed what was one of my biggest bookings of 2019.

LET ME SHARE ANOTHER EXAMPLE OF THAT PROCESS, BUT WITH A COMPANY I RECENTLY TRAINED ...

I was hired by a recruitment company to train their team. After spending some time with the Manager before training, I was told that their competitive edge was that they were able to save their customers up to 80% off their recruitment costs. A very big and bold offer.

During the training, when we were brainstorming article ideas, the sales team came up with some really strong ideas, including 'Why Recruitment Is Too Expensive In 2020', 'Are Recruiters Charging Too Much?' and 'Top 10 Tips to Recruit the Best Staff in 2020'. The next day one of the reps went with 'Are Recruiters Charging Too Much?' and put together their first article.

The article was packed with great insight, some statistics they had sourced and some really strong original ideas. At the end of the article they had included information about what they did, and how they had helped companies recently save a lot of money on their recruitment costs.

A few days after publishing it, they received a message from someone who enjoyed the article and was interested to see if they could save money on the thousands they were spending every year on recruitment.

It took a couple of weeks to close the sale after receiving the lead, but they won it.

The key points to remember are:

1) Write content that is valuable to your prospect.
2) Make the content engaging and enjoyable to read.
3) Have a strong CTA (call to action) at the end to show people how you can help.
4) Include your contact details.

LinkedIn Article Structure

A good LinkedIn article needs to take people on a journey, your goal being to get them to read as much of it as possible, ideally all of it. To do this you need to structure it the right way. I've found a good article includes these key components:

1) Introduction/Opening Hook – First you need to hook people in with a strong opening sentence or paragraph. This should be connected to the title and written to capture their attention and create desire and intrigue to read the article.

2) The Story – After you've hooked them in, you then want to start telling the story. Take them on a journey and break the story into easy to digest parts. Break the story up, if you can, with quotes, media or links to help drive engagement.

3) The Conclusion/Summary – After telling the story or working through the tips you then want to summarise your article, bringing it to a nice conclusion or opening it up for debate or asking the reader a question.

4) CTA (call to action) – Next you want to direct the reader as to what you'd like them to do next. This could be directing them to other articles, a website or content engagement.

5) About the author – Finally, you can tell the reader a little bit about yourself, written in a similar style to your LinkedIn summary. This is a great place to discuss what it is you do and how you help people, and how people can get in touch with you.

Example blog

The Sad Truth of Sales In 2019

Sales Manager: Give them a call

Sales Rep: I've emailed them

Sales Manager: Be quicker to call them...

Sales Rep: I've texted them as well

Sales Manager: JUST CALL THEM

Sales Rep: I'll send another email

JUST PICK UP THE PHONE AND CALL!
Daniel Disney on LinkedIn
February 14, 2019

There is a serious problem plaguing sales teams across the world ...

It's like a dangerous and contagious sales virus infecting salespeople old and young ...

Left unchecked it could destroy any chances of success ...

What is this problem you ask?

THE FEAR OF THE PHONE!

I saw this problem first-hand recently at one of my training sessions.

Now those of you who will look at my profile will see that I'm a Social Selling/LinkedIn Sales trainer, so my focus is ironically around utilising social media to sell. HOWEVER, even I know that the phone is a very powerful sales tool, I'm not one of those social selling trainers trying to discourage people from using the phone, personally I encourage it.

Anyway, during this training session I had mentioned seeing someone post on LinkedIn just one week ago that they were actually in the market for the product that this particular company actually sold!

One of those 'Can anyone in my network recommend a provider of X or Y please' posts that you see ...

Now because I had seen this post, I tagged in one of the directors from this company and suggested they reach out as I knew they were great at what they did. Unfortunately the director wasn't active on LinkedIn, so they didn't action this genuinely hot lead opportunity.

Luckily one of the sales team were way ahead and had seen that the director was tagged and so acted on this amazing opportunity! They had written a comment, sent a connection request and after the connection was accepted, sent a nice little message saying that they would love to discuss their requirement in more detail.

Now in the world of Social Selling, this is an amazing start!!

There will be loads of sales reps who wouldn't have seen this post in the first place or thought to proactively act on it like they had done.

It had been just over one week from them seeing, connecting and messaging this prospect, so I asked the sales rep (the whole team was now listening at this point) 'What happened next then ......?'

This was their reply.

They turned to me and very proudly said ...

  'I'm just waiting for them to reply'.

Cue my genuine reaction:

I'M SORRY, WHAT??!

You are <u>waiting</u> for them to reply? It's been over a week and you're still waiting for THEM to reply?

I go on to explain that the person who wrote on LinkedIn that they needed something probably had over 100+ sales-people comment on the post, 100+ new connections, 100+ messages into their inbox etc. It is hugely overwhelming and very difficult to reply to every single person.

The reality, unfortunately, is that most of those sales reps who comment, connect and message will also be sat there WAITING for a reply.

A reply that for most of them (if not all of them) will never come.

My advice to this particular sales rep ...

Just Pick Up the Phone and Call Them!

I can GUARANTEE you very few salespeople that jump onto these LinkedIn posts will pick up the phone and give the prospect a call.

And that is the sad truth of sales in 2019 …

The Sad Truth of Sales In 2019

Sales Manager: Give them a call
Sales Rep: I've emailed them
Sales Manager: Be quicker to call them...
Sales Rep: I've texted them as well
Sales Manager: JUST CALL THEM
Sales Rep: I'll send another email

There are too many salespeople, both old and young, that are scared to pick up the phone.

I mean look, you know it must be bad if a Social Selling trainer is complaining about people not using the phone right??!!!!

Forget debates about cold calling vs. social selling

Forget debates about millennials being scared of the phone

Here is the simple truth …

PEOPLE ARE STILL ANSWERING CALLS

As long as people are using the phone, it will remain a powerful sales tool.

Why are people scared of the phone though?

This fear comes from a few areas.

The first is fear of rejection. When you send an email, you're hidden behind your computer. When you comment on a LinkedIn post, if they just don't reply that rejection isn't as personal. However, when you're on the phone to someone, that rejection can be harsh and uncomfortable.

Well guess what, often a lot of what we want in life is on the other side of uncomfortable.

Everything you've ever wanted
is on the other side of fear.

Look at the situation above ...

If you let fear of the phone control you, chances are you'll miss that sale. If you keep looking to send an email, send a text, send a LinkedIn message as a way of avoiding the phone, you'll miss opportunities.

It's not to say that email, text, social etc aren't good methods, they 100% are.

It's when you use them to cover up fear of picking up the phone OR you wait too long for replies that will never come that it becomes a problem.

This is where the other reasons people are scared ...

They fear what they don't know. They fear having to learn something new.

A lot of salespeople don't know how to use the phone success-fully, and it's scary having to learn something new.

Trust me there are equally as many salespeople who are scared to use social media. They'll hide behind making constant calls to people who will never answer or return them to avoid learning how to use LinkedIn.

It's the OTHER sad truth of sales in 2019 ....

The OTHER Sad Truth of Sales In 2019

Sales Manager: Try using LinkedIn
Sales Rep: I've called them
Sales Manager: But they didn't answer?
Sales Rep: I'll call them again
Sales Manager: They've blocked you now
Sales Rep: I'll try calling them again

Fear is crippling salespeople and sales teams but it can be overcome. This problem can be CURED! You need to understand one thing first ...

Working in sales ISN'T easy.

The whole reason that salespeople get paid a commission for what they do is because they have to work hard and overcome challenges to win each sale. You don't get paid for making calls. You don't get paid for commenting on someone's LinkedIn post. You get paid for WINNING and closing sales. Everything else is part of the process to winning those sales.

The ONE question you need to ask yourself ...

HOW BAD DO YOU WANT THE SALE?

The salespeople out there that want the sale MORE are the ones who don't let fear hold them back. They will pick up the phone if they need to, they'll jump on LinkedIn, they'll get in their car and drive there if the need to!

- The phone is not dead
- Social Selling is not dead
- Email is not dead
- Sending letters is not dead
- Networking is not dead

If you're working in sales right now you have the single BEST opportunity that ANY salesperson has ever had. There have never EVER been more opportunities to reach prospects and customers than there are right now.

Salespeople have the opportunity to leverage SO MANY tools which gives you the opportunity to reach more people.

Don't let fear of rejection hold you back.

Don't let fear of what you don't know hold you back.

If you REALLY want the sale, you'll let nothing stand in your way!

So go out there today, look at your opportunities and look at all the amazing tools at your disposal. Be creative, be persistent, be passionate and try harder than you've ever tried to go out there and help people solve more problems with your product.

If you enjoyed this blog please click LIKE and click SHARE to share it with your network, thank you!

If you enjoyed this post please take time to read some of my other recent posts.

Stop Micro-Managing Salespeople

The MUST-HAVE Sales Books of 2018

The 10 Things That Will NEVER Change In Sales

How To Make Cold Calling Fun!

About the author:

Daniel Disney is one of the world's leading sales, social selling and LinkedIn experts. With over 15 years sales experience, Daniel has mastered how to use social media to generate exceptional results, both in social engagement and in revenue generated.

Daniel is a highly in-demand international keynote sales speaker, is the UK's leading sales blogger and is also the Founder and Owner of LinkedIn's most popular sales publication, The Daily Sales. With an audience of over 450,000+ followers and growing by thousands each week, his content reaches millions of salespeople far and wide.

To inquire about Daniel keynoting or speaking at your company or event, or to find out more about his 1-day LinkedIn/Social Selling Masterclass please email contact@ thedailysales.net.

CHAPTER 17

CREATING VIRAL CONTENT ON LINKEDIN

'Good content can reach hundreds or even thousands of people; viral content can reach millions'.

Creating good content will make a big difference but creating viral content on LinkedIn can help you take it to a whole new level.

Important Note: Viral content doesn't guarantee success and can easily cause harm if done the wrong way. I've seen many people on LinkedIn try to create viral content just for the sake of the engagement. The problem is if you share bland content with no relevance to you, your industry or your product, whilst it may generate you some better engagement, it will do very little else and may in fact scare away potential customers.

The key is to create viral content that is relevant. If you can do that, you'll truly benefit from it.

There is no set number that defines what classes as viral; different people will have different viewpoints of which number it should be. It also varies massively on different social media networks. Facebook, for example, tends to view content as viral if it achieves tens to hundreds of thousands of likes. On YouTube you're looking at multiple millions of views to class as viral.

The three stages of viral content on LinkedIn

After studying content on LinkedIn for nearly 10 years now, in my personal and professional opinion I would say that any post that generates above 200 likes can be classed as viral.

Now, because there are different levels of engagement on LinkedIn, I've created three stages of viral content that I believe helps differentiate them.

Stage One – Most posts on LinkedIn tend to get between zero and 25 likes. You then get good performing posts hitting 25–100 likes and strong posts getting up to 200. This is why I class 200 and above Stage 1 viral.

Stage Two – You then get posts that hit 1,000+ likes, which is what I call Stage 2 viral. This is quite a rare achievement and one that very few achieve.

Stage Three – You then get the even rarer posts that generate 10,000+ likes, which is Stage 3 viral. These posts reach millions of people and are the highest form of viral on LinkedIn.

Over my social/digital selling career I've been fortunate to create and share multiple Stage 1, 2 and 3 viral posts and, in this chapter, I'm going to share with you everything I know about how to do it and what makes a post go viral on LinkedIn.

Let me start by giving you an example:

The Daily Sales Game of Sales!! Follow The Daily Sales for more!

il. Organic ⊘
Targeted to: All Followers

1,830,426	79,070	9,169	4.82%
impressions	clicks	interactions	engagement

One of my best performing memes was this wonderful Game of Thrones meme. Firstly, I have shared well over 15 Game of Thrones sales memes over the years. Most of them achieved around 100,000–200,000 impressions. I've also shared many 'first day/last day' sales memes over the years, achieving the same level of impressions.

What then, do you think, made this one generate just shy of 2,000,000 impressions??

When I ask this in my training sessions I often get these guesses:

- Because it's Jon Snow?
- Because it's funny?
- Because everyone likes Game of Thrones?

Here is the real reason ...

It's because I posted this the DAY AFTER the episode pictured in the bottom picture was aired. This was during series five, which was around when Game of Thrones was at the peak of its popularity. (Many fans feel it went downhill after then, although I must say I enjoyed every episode from series one to eight!)

Not only was it a meme that everyone in sales can relate to, but it included images that were super-relevant at that time. Let me share another example:

10 Things That Will NEVER Change In Sales

Published on March 9, 2017   ✎ Edit article | ⬚ View stats

One of my LinkedIn articles went viral in 2017, generating over 19,000 likes. The article itself wasn't very different to the other 300+ articles that I have written; however, something caused it to go viral.

The secret, just like the Game of Thrones meme I shared before, was posting it at the right time. I wrote and published this article when the cold calling/social selling debate reached a crazy point.

At the time, traditional sales experts were naming and shaming social selling experts, and vice versa. It was crazy, the posts going back and forth started to get extremely aggressive, bordering on unprofessional.

What I saw as an opportunity wasn't to take a side, but instead to write something that would bring both sides together, which was where the idea of 'The 10 Things That Will NEVER Change In Sales' came from.

That is what, in my experience, is the key to viral content on LinkedIn:

The right subject.
The right format.
The right time.

First, you need to find the right subject. This can be something relevant, something controversial, something popular, etc. Then you need to choose the right format for it. That could be a short text post, long text post, quote, meme, video, etc. Finally you need to post it at the right time; the moment where it will make the most impact on the wider LinkedIn audience.

VIRAL CONTENT TOP TIPS

Look through your LinkedIn feed, LinkedIn hashtags or Twitter hashtags to see which subjects are trending and popular right now.

Listen to LinkedIn experts to see which format of content on LinkedIn is performing best right now (feel free to message me and ask).

Try to find a way of connecting the subject to your customers to make it relevant to them.

Try to get industry influencers or key pages to share or engage with your content. This puts it in front of a large audience, helping drive higher engagement.

PART 6
PERSONAL BRANDING

'People buy from people, we know that. Your personal brand is your opportunity to show your prospects and customers that you are a human being, and not just another salesperson trying to sell something'.

CHAPTER 18

BUILDING AN INDUSTRY-LEADING PERSONAL BRAND

The term 'personal brand' is tossed around a lot at the moment.

Lots of experts shouting that everyone needs a personal brand, that all salespeople need to invest in their personal brand, etc. But what does it mean? What IS a personal brand? And why should you care about yours?

I'm going to give you a few examples in this chapter about why and how a personal brand is important; however, I want to start with this one.

Throughout my early sales career, I spent a lot of time introducing myself to prospects.

The process of doing so would often take up the first 10–15 minutes of every meeting, or the first few minutes of every cold call.

'Hi, my name is Daniel Disney, I work for X company. What we do here is blah blah blah', you get the idea.

It is what most salespeople have to do all over the world, and whenever I get approached by a salesperson this is often how the conversation starts.

After a few months of being active on LinkedIn during my early social selling days, without realising, I started to build a personal brand. I had been sharing content nearly every day, growing my audience and engagement along the way.

One day I went to attend a prospect meeting that I had booked a few weeks ago. Now, usually when I walked in, the conversation would start as I mentioned earlier, 'Hi, my name is Daniel Disney and I work for…'. However, this did not happen that day …

As I walked in, before I even had chance to sit down, the prospect jumped up and said:

> 'Ah Daniel, it's great to see you today. I absolutely LOVED that blog that you wrote last week! You really hit the nail on the head about some of the challenges this industry is facing. Take a seat, I'm excited to hear about what you might be able to do for us'.

Wow, I thought. I'd just jumped several steps in the process. They knew who I was, I had already earned a level of trust and respect, and instead of looking at me as just another salesperson, I was on their level, they had accepted me.

That is the power of a personal brand.

THE C-LEVEL IMPACT ...

Here is another example I wanted to share. This one has literally happened as I'm writing this book. As I mentioned at the start, along with selling my Social Selling training and speaking, I also sell advertisement packages for The Daily Sales.

My ICP for these are usually marketing leaders (VP Marketing, Marketing Director, Marketing Manager); however, I always make sure I not only connect with others within their teams and the business, but I also connect with the CEO/MD/Owner.

These are often high-level C-Suite executives at the top of the corporate tree, people whom I would regard as THE most difficult to connect with on LinkedIn.

Whilst writing this book I have been prospecting a few potential companies utilising everything you're reading about. With one of the companies I am prospecting, I sent a connection request to the CEO. This is the CEO of a global multi-million turnover company, with hundreds of employees and growing fast.

Here is the personalised message that I sent them:

Hi (Name),

I love what you're doing at (insert company).

I'd love to connect,

Kind

Regards,

Dan

Nothing complex, not a sales pitch, just a nice, simple connection request message.

Around one hour later they accepted my connection request. Great! However, they also replied to my personalised connection request with this message:

Hi Dan,

Your reputation precedes you. Looking forward to getting to know you,

Kind

Regards,

CEO

Once again, that is the power of a personal brand. Not just building an industry reputation, not just giving a good impression to your prospective customers, but also to the highest-level people within their businesses.

Let's not forget that it is often these people who ultimately hold the budget. Whilst my customer and main contact may be the Marketing Manager or Marketing Director, they will sometimes have to run decisions past the CEO/MD or Finance Director, especially for large contracts.

Building a personal brand that reaches these people can be a huge advantage in winning opportunities and also building extremely strong, long-lasting relationships with companies.

WHAT IS A PERSONAL BRAND?

One of the easiest ways I can describe a personal brand is to compare it to your diet.

You've no doubt heard the saying, '**You are what you eat**', which is used to highlight that if you constantly eat bad, unhealthy food, then that is what you'll be, unhealthy. If you fill your body with bad food, it will directly impact how effectively your body operates.

In the world of social media, your personal brand is just like that.

Your personal brand is made up of your social media activity, reputation, knowledge and experience. So just like in the world of health you are what you eat, in the world of social media and your personal brand you are what you like, comment on, share and create!

DO YOU NEED A PERSONAL BRAND?

There is one universal truth that we know in sales …

PEOPLE BUY FROM PEOPLE THEY KNOW, LIKE AND TRUST

Think about it, when was the last time you bought from someone you didn't trust? It doesn't happen. If we don't trust someone, we won't give them our money.

Your personal brand can be a huge advantage in building trust, building relationships and giving value, which is why it's become a big part of modern-day selling. These are all crucial aspects of successful sales.

Before social media came around, salespeople would spend hours, days and weeks building trust, building relationships and giving value. Now salespeople can do it in far less time simply sitting behind their computer screen. Obviously, it's then enhanced when a social media personal brand is matched with physical meetings, phone calls, video calls, attending events, etc.

HOW DO YOU BUILD A PERSONAL BRAND?

A personal brand is mainly built up from the content you share and the engagement you provide on a regular basis. If, for example, you share one piece of content per week, your personal brand is unlikely to be as strong or as popular as someone sharing content three times per week. There are two very simple keys to growing a successful personal brand:

CONSISTENCY AND VALUE

If you want to build a strong, respected personal brand, you need to be consistent in providing value. It's that simple. Both are key to success, but both are also how you can lose a personal brand. I've seen some amazing people share consistent valuable content, and within just a few weeks they are getting attention from all over the world.

They do that for several months, and then for reasons of their own, they stop sharing content as often. When you stop sharing content for more than a week, your personal brand will shrink. I've seen amazing personal brands, with people getting thousands of likes on their posts, disappear for mere weeks or months, and then when they reappear they struggle to get 20 likes on their posts.

BUILD A PERSONAL BRAND IN JUST 15 MINUTES PER DAY

To really see results, I have broken the 15 minutes into three, five-minute activities. Again, to see results they really need to be carried out on a regular, consistent, daily basis. That is part of why this can work.

1 – Grow your network (five minutes)

The first stage is to start growing your network each and every day. Spend the first five minutes adding potential prospects, adding people within prospective companies or adding people relevant to your industry. LinkedIn will automatically recommend people for you, or you can do a couple of quick searches.

If you can add at least 10 connections each day, that's 300 each month and 3,600 in a year. If you're slowly filling your network with prospects, you'll then increase the chance of generating inbound enquiries plus you'll create the opportunity to start outbound conversations with them via messaging.

2 – Share and create content (five minutes)

Five minutes isn't a lot of time in the world of content, but it's enough to start. My advice would be to subscribe to as many industry-relevant news channels as possible. This way you'll get the latest industry news direct to your inbox every day. Finding a good article and clicking the LinkedIn icon to share it takes a couple of minutes, plus adding your own thoughts takes you up to the five.

Creating a nice post can easily be done in five minutes. Whether it's a quick photo of yourself in a specific location with some writing attached, a quick story, some insight or even a short three-minute video, you can easily create something impactful in five minutes. My advice is share two bits of news each week and create three posts each week.

By sharing content every day, you'll firstly start to build a personal brand. Done right, your content has the potential to generate inbound leads and you have the opportunity to use the engagement or content to start conversations with prospects.

3 – Social post engagement (five minutes)

The final five minutes should be invested in social engagement. This includes everything from liking a few posts to commenting on a few posts. Again, this should be a mixture of engaging on your prospects' content and industry-relevant content.

The aim is to make sure your name is out there every day. By engaging on your prospects' posts you'll earn credibility, build relationships and hopefully generate opportunities. By engaging on industry-relevant posts you'll start to build your personal brand, which will be noticed by prospects and peers.

And there it is: three simple five-minute activities, just 15 minutes per day that, when done on a regular basis, has the potential to generate some pretty awesome results.

Now you could spend 20 minutes a day, 30 minutes or more. The key is to make sure you are investing that time and not wasting it.

PERSONAL BRAND TOP TIPS

Think before you post and engage. Everything you do online impacts your personal brand, so think before you do and make sure what you do aligns to your brand.

Find the right balance between personal and brand. You need a good balance of corporate/professionally relevant content and engagement along with personal content and engagement. I would recommend 70–80% professionally relevant content and 20–30% personal content.

Consistency is key, so think about scheduling time daily/weekly to do your personal brand building activities.

Adopt a GIVING mentality. Don't create content for engagement, create it to give value. Don't engage on people's content to get your name out, do it to provide value.

Be authentic and be you. Share your stories, share your experiences and share your thoughts and opinions.

CHAPTER 19

GENERATING LEADS FROM LINKEDIN

Whilst you should see that there are many ways you can generate leads throughout each chapter and section of this book, I want to run through some of the highest performing lead generation techniques on LinkedIn.

CONTENT AND PERSONAL BRAND

The biggest generator of leads for me, and for the people that I train, coach and consult, is content and personal brand. I've put them together because they go side by side. If you're sharing good content, then you're building a good personal brand, and if you're building a good personal brand, it's usually because you're sharing good content!

In my experience, a LinkedIn article is one of the best forms of content for lead generation because it is one of the only forms of content where you can include an 'about you' section that goes into detail about what you offer and how they can get in touch. There aren't any other forms of content that allow you to do this unless the post itself is of an advertising style, which hopefully you'll know by now is not something to do a lot of.

Other forms of content also work well as lead generators when you create good, engaging, value-packed posts that, in a very subtle way, highlight how you help and the results you can help people achieve.

Building a good personal brand is also a super-powerful lead generation source. Building an audience and a credible/trusted reputation in your industry can build a constant source of leads if done right.

Remember this comes down to three key things:

– Grow your audience with your target prospects or people who may recommend you to your target prospects. Grow it every single day.

- Engage with industry-relevant posts, and ideally high performing industry-relevant posts to get your name out there on a regular and consistent basis.
- Create your own authentic and industry-relevant content on a consistent basis.

Don't forget that not only will a good personal brand generate inbound leads for you, but done right it will also prompt and encourage other people to tag you into potential hot leads for people posting about your product or service or through more direct introductions and referrals.

YOUR PROFILE

This then leads to one of the other key areas of LinkedIn that works well as a lead generator, your LinkedIn profile. Creating great content is good, but a percentage of the traffic consuming that content will then be directed to your profile. If it's bad, you'll lose them, but if it is good, you stand a chance of converting them into an inbound or outbound lead.

Make your profile customer facing and focus on how you can help them, not what you can sell them. The core areas that provide the biggest impact in lead generation are your profile background/banner image and your summary, with your profile photo also having a small influential factor as well.

INTERVIEWS AND GUEST POSTS

Another great way to generate leads is to do interviews and guest on other people's content. This could involve being a guest on an industry-relevant podcast, writing a guest blog for an industry publication, doing a LinkedIn LIVE interview with someone, anything that gets you in front of someone else's audience.

This has been another of the strongest generators of inbound leads for my businesses over the years. A few things to consider though: firstly, try to find audiences that are relevant to you. I'm invited onto many different podcasts and shows, but the reality is not all of them are valuable to me. As harsh as it may sound, sometimes you'll be better off saying no. Your time is valuable and it's important you allocate it to activities that have a good chance of generating results and helping you progress.

Secondly, you want to make sure the interview or guest contribution presents you in the right way. This is the equivalent of standing on stage in front of a totally new audience with the hope of them following you afterwards and some of them coming to you with opportunities. You need to make a good impression and try to make sure that the subject and conversation allow you to present yourself in the best way possible.

Finally, it's also a great piece of content for you to share to your audience! Whilst your main benefit is reaching a new audience, it also has a huge benefit of being valuable to your own audience.

For example, if you get interviewed by an industry expert, some people will view it as you being endorsed by that expert and so will see you as more credible. Equally, sharing content showing you're heavily involved in your industry will encourage people in your own audience to take you seriously and potentially reach out to you.

LinkedIn can be a very powerful lead-generating machine with some businesses and salespeople generating 100% of their pipeline and target through it.

Whilst this book covers many ways to do this, these are the ones that have proven to be the most valuable methods of lead generation for me.

PART 7
SALES STRATEGY

CHAPTER 20

ACCOUNT-BASED MARKETING, MANAGING ACCOUNTS & BUILDING DIGITAL RELATIONSHIPS

Many years ago, account management in sales was mainly done with a three-month, six-month or 12-month catch-up call. After the initial deal was closed, salespeople would call after a select period to see how things were going (whilst also looking for any other sales opportunities).

LinkedIn has brought a whole new world of opportunity to account management. Instead of only having these scheduled catch-up calls, LinkedIn and social media allow you to build your relationship with your customers every single day.

By connecting with them on social media, you have the chance to engage with their content, clicking like and adding comments. You get to give value to them by sharing your own content. You get to follow what they are doing from their posts and they get to follow what you're doing from your posts.

Not long ago I was delivering training for a large company, and as I arrived and grabbed a coffee with the VP of sales, the first question they asked was '*How was the Philippines?*' (The week prior I had been in the Philippines keynoting at a sales kick-off.) How did they know this? Because I had posted about it on social media.

It builds a much stronger relationship; they enjoy getting to see what you're doing, and you get to enjoy seeing what they're doing.

There are a few great ways to do this:

1) Share content regularly. Share what you're doing, share events you're attending, industry news that you're reading, books that you're reading, stories, insights, etc.
2) Engage with their content. Click like on their posts and write comments with your thoughts. Think about how good it feels when someone clicks LIKE or writes a COMMENT on your posts, it feels awesome!! Now imagine how they will feel; it's a great opportunity to make them feel appreciated and supported.

NOTE – Don't engage with EVERY SINGLE ONE of their posts, that's a little stalkery. ☺

3) Connect on other platforms as well as LinkedIn (where relevant and appropriate). I am connected to some of my longest standing customers not just on LinkedIn, but on Facebook, Twitter and even Instagram.

4) Use video and audio messaging to send update messages or catch-up messages that are more engaging than written ones.

CHAPTER 21

MULTI-TOUCH SELLING

There are a few terms for it, multi-touch, combo, Omni-channel, modern, digital, it all means the same thing: using ALL of the tools available to communicate with your prospects and customers.

In this book I've shown you how to leverage LinkedIn in all of the ways that you can. But I can't stress enough that to get the most out of LinkedIn, you will need to use other platforms as well.

This includes:

- Phone calls
- Texts
- Video messages
- Video calls
- Emails
- Voicemails
- Letters
- Gifts
- Referrals
- Door knocking

Every sales strategy, whether you're working for yourself, working as part of a small sales team or a large enterprise company, should include a multi-touch sales approach.

I have had many deals won that have been 100% created and closed on LinkedIn, without the use of any other platform. However, the majority of my business will involve at least one other, if not several other, platforms as well.

The most common sequence/cadence for me is to create the opportunity via LinkedIn, getting to the point in a LinkedIn message conversation that the prospect wants to receive more information or a quote via email, or to arrange a phone call or video call to discuss in more detail.

The formal proposal is then usually sent via email or DocuSign, followed by a preparation call or video chat before delivery.

To this day, I still use all of the items on that list. I send gifts to prospects, I send letters, I generate business through referrals, I generate business through texts and even knock on the occasional door if I spot a potential prospect whilst I'm out working.

If there are any methods that are on that list that you are not confident in, then I would highly recommend learning about them. Seek formal training, read books, consume content and go out there and start practicing.

Modern salespeople need to be multi-tool trained and multi-tool confident.

CHAPTER 22

LINKEDIN TOOLS, TECHNOLOGY & SOFTWARE

There are many tools out there that can support your digital and social selling efforts via LinkedIn. They can help you with content creation, message recording, video/photo equipment, posting automation and more.

There is a fine line between being smart with technology and trying to take too many shortcuts ...

There are tools, software and third party organisations that offer to automate or do some key LinkedIn and Social Selling tasks for you. My advice would be to be cautious with these.

The best content on LinkedIn is the content created by YOU, not something by someone else and shared by you.

The best messages are the messages written by YOU and personalised with truly relevant information and real authenticity, not a bland template scheduled to be sent out to everyone.

There are tools that will help you sell better on LinkedIn, and there are tools that claim to sell for you on LinkedIn. I'd recommend using tools that help you sell better.

Here are the ones that I am currently using right now:

Buffer

I use www.buffer.com to schedule content in advance. I have also used, and would also recommend, Hootsuite, which does the same.

Canva

I use www.canva.com to create a lot of the content that I share, as well as for creating LinkedIn banners.

Vidyard

I use www.vidyard.com to record, edit and share great videos, both for content and for prospecting.

Shield Analytics

I use www.shieldapp.ai to see deeper analytics of my content on LinkedIn and what's working best.

Mematic

I use Mematic on my iPhone to create memes.

Zubtitle

I use www.zubtitle.com to add subtitles/captions to my videos.

Quicktime Player and iMovie

I use Quicktime Player and iMovie on my MacBook Pro to record and edit videos.

Logitech C920S

The camera I use for my videos, webinars, LinkedIn LIVEs and podcasts is a Logitech C920S, which is fantastic and is as good now as it was when I bought it three years ago.

Snowball Ice

I use a Snowball Ice microphone to record and capture all of my audio.

Docooler Ring Light

I have a Docooler Ring Light to ensure lighting is as good as possible during videos.

LinkedIn Sales Navigator

I use LinkedIn Sales Navigator to help with all of my social selling activities.

CRM

I would also recommend utilising the CRM that you have to track and record social selling insights and results. CRMs that I have used and would recommend include HubSpot, Gold Vision CRM, Salesforce, Microsoft Dynamics, Pipedrive, SET for Business and Freshworks CRM.

Lead Forensics

I'd also recommend using www.leadforensics.com to track who is viewing your website, which you can then integrate into your sales and social selling strategy.

Sales Engagement

There are some amazing sales engagement platforms that help streamline your sales and social selling activities. I'd highly recommend checking out Outreach, VanillaSoft and Salesloft.

CHAPTER 23

MEASURING RESULTS ON LINKEDIN & YOUR SSI SCORE

After applying what you've learned in this book, you're going to want to track the results that it achieves. Are your messages creating opportunities? Is your content generating leads? How many sales came from LinkedIn?

There are two key ways that you can (and should) measure success with LinkedIn and Social Selling.

Your SSI Score

LinkedIn has their own official social selling scoring system called the SSI score (Social Selling Index). This is completely free to use for anyone, although it is included and accessible through your Sales Navigator account. You simply follow a link and LinkedIn will give you a score out of 100 on how well you're doing based on their key metrics:

1: ESTABLISH YOUR PROFESSIONAL BRAND

Complete your profile with the customer in mind. Become a thought-leader by publishing meaningful posts.

2: FIND THE RIGHT PEOPLE

Identify better prospects in less time using efficient search and research tools.

3: ENGAGE WITH INSIGHTS

Discover and share conversation-worthy updates to create and grow relationships.

4: BUILD RELATIONSHIPS

Strengthen your network by connecting and establishing trust with decision makers.

Social Selling Index – Today

Your Social Selling Index (SSI) measures how effective you are at establishing your professional brand, finding the right people, engaging with insights, and building relationships. It is updated daily. Learn more

Establish your professional brand		25
	0	25
Find the right people	18.72	
	0	25
Engage with insights	18.8	
	0	25
Build relationships		25

You can get your SSI score right here:

I've met a lot of sales teams and salespeople that only use the SSI score to measure their social selling activities. There is a big problem with this in that your SSI doesn't actually measure selling!

This is where the second part of measurement comes in:

Sales Tracking

It is equally, if not more important, to track the real sales metrics being generated by LinkedIn and social/digital selling. This should include:

How many leads generated this week/month/quarter/year from
LinkedIn/Social Selling
How many opportunities created
How many deals closed
How much revenue generated
How many prospecting messages sent

Unfortunately, most of these will need to be tracked manually, although this is where using a good CRM properly really helps. I'd also recommend creating a spreadsheet or simple piece of recordkeeping software to track and measure these results.

When you combine your LinkedIn SSI score with your sales tracking results, then you get a truly comprehensive scoring for your LinkedIn and social selling activities.

CHAPTER 24

LINKEDIN SALES NAVIGATOR TIPS

LinkedIn Sales Navigator is an *AMAZING* sales tool when used right.

The problem for many salespeople and sales teams is that their company buys it for them, but then doesn't provide any comprehensive training on how to use it. It's like buying gym membership but not being given an induction on how to use the machines.

To help you get started I've pulled together 11 ways that you can generate leads and start to get the best out of Sales Navigator.

(If you're keen to learn how to really get the most out of Sales Navigator, I run regular virtual training sessions. Check out www.danieldisney.online to find out when the next ones are running.)

1) 'VIEW SIMILAR' PROSPECTS

Sales Navigator makes it easy to find similar prospects with the 'view similar' button. Once you find an ideal prospect, simply select the dropdown and Sales Navigator will populate results with similar job titles and backgrounds at other companies.

Each individual prospect will generate their own list, so you can end up creating loads of new leads and prospects each time. The qualified ones can then be added to your prospect list and worked along with your other prospects.

2) USE 'BLUEBIRD' SEARCHES

A Bluebird search on Navigator is where you find people that worked at companies that you've sold to before. You can find them in whichever new roles and companies they may now be in and reignite that relationship. They may be new in a role and so open to taking on new suppliers, or they may remember working with you and be keen to continue that.

3) SEARCH FOR CONTENT KEYWORDS

You can search for people on Sales Navigator who have used industry keywords. This will help you find active prospects and also direct you to a piece of content that you can then use to start a conversation with them.

You may also find potential buying signals, news relevant to the prospect or information that may help you during the sales process. You can also save the search so that you can come back to it the following day.

4) LOOK AT YOUR 'SHARED EXPERIENCES'

This is the same principle as the traditional sales technique of looking around your prospect's office for things in common or conversation starter opportunities. For example, you might see a picture of their family, maybe a sports team or sports trophy, or maybe there are some books you recognise on the bookshelf.

LinkedIn Sales Navigator is doing this for you with its 'Shared Experiences' filter. It will show you people who share something with you, for example, a group that you may both be in. This then gives you an amazing opportunity to use that to start a warmer conversation.

5) FIND THE MOST ENGAGED PROSPECTS

It can be hard to tell how active a prospect is on LinkedIn, and that can have a huge impact on whether they respond to you. Sales Navigator is helping with this by allowing you to filter the most active prospects in your searches.

By clicking on 'Posted on LinkedIn in the past 30 days', you're going to find the most active prospects on the list. You can then find what they posted and use that as a conversation opener, or use it to engage with their content and build the foundations of the relationship before directly talking to them.

6) LET SALES NAVIGATOR FIND YOU LEADS

Possibly the easiest way to generate leads with Sales Navigator is to get it to do it for you! The key to this is to ensure you put as much information as you can into your profile and settings to help it find you the best possible leads. The less information you put in, the weaker the leads that will come out.

I would recommend checking this on a regular basis as there will be new prospects coming onto LinkedIn, new people into roles, etc. so it's worth keeping a regular eye on this list.

7) LOOK FOR PEOPLE IN NEW ROLES

It's a well-known fact that people new into roles are often more open to changing suppliers compared to those who have been in the role for a long time. They want to make a good impression and add their own stamp on the role.

Sales Navigator will show you the people who have changed jobs in the past 90 days, who are potentially very warm prospects for you to approach. You can congratulate them on their new role and use it to start a nicer conversation.

8) LOOK AT WHO IS VIEWING YOUR PROFILE

Possibly one of the most powerful and under-used social selling techniques, checking who is viewing your profile can open up loads of sales opportunities. On the free LinkedIn account, unfortunately, it will only show the most recent three or four people who have viewed your profile. However, with Sales Navigator it will show you ALL of them.

Scroll through and find the ones that potentially qualify as prospects, connect and then use the fact they viewed your profile to open a conversation. This one in particular has helped me create a lot of sales opportunities.

9) LOOK FOR COMMON POINTS

Not only can you see everyone who has viewed your profile on Sales Navigator (one of the features that really justifies its price), but it will also show you people with whom you have things in common.

Once again, this is an amazing way to find things you can use to open or progress a conversation with them. It may direct you to companies you follow, groups you're in, or mutual connections who might be able to refer you, etc.

10) SAVE SEARCHES TO SAVE TIME

Manually searching every day takes time, but with Sales Navigator you can save searches so that you can jump straight into them. That time saved can then be invested into finding and contacting even more people to hopefully generate more opportunities.

11) EXTEND YOUR INMAIL LIMIT

'Open Profiles' don't count towards your InMail limit, so keep an eye out for people who have this type of profile. This will allow you to send MORE InMails than usual, potentially opening more doors and creating more opportunities.

Now don't get me wrong, not many decision makers will have open profiles, I know that. However, there is a chance that other people within their companies will have open profiles, and you can use them to try and get through to the decision maker.

CHAPTER 25

THE FUTURE OF SOCIAL & DIGITAL SELLING

Over the years that I have been using LinkedIn it has changed tremendously. It is constantly changing everything from the features that it has and the way that it looks to the way the algorithm works.

Here are some of my thoughts on what I think is in store for the future of LinkedIn and social selling:

1) THE CONTINUED RISE OF VIDEO

Video is going to be the next big change in sales. At the time of writing this book very few sales teams and salespeople are leveraging video in their sales process. This will most definitely change over the coming years until it is as normal as picking up the phone.

The sales teams that are ahead of the curve at the moment are now building video pods within their office spaces. These are little areas that allow salespeople to record top-quality video messages and video content.

2) SOCIAL ENABLEMENT TOOLS

LinkedIn has always been very protective over its data, making it difficult for external software platforms to provide additional services much like many sales enablement and engagement tools do.

I believe that this will change, and more and more software platforms, tools and CRMs will get greater access to LinkedIn, helping salespeople become more efficient and effective with using it to sell.

3) THE RISE OF EMOJIS/MEMES AND GIFS!

I come from a time when none of the above were EVER used in sales, so even for me it is still quite strange to consider these a part of selling. However, they are now a big part of our world. And because they are a part of many of our customers' worlds, they are now a part of the sales world.

As younger generations rise up the hierarchy, the use of these types of media will become an even bigger part of corporate and sales communication. I have customers that send me memes, customers that use emojis in their emails and messages and customers that use GIFs.

My rule of thumb with this is to let them use them first. You wouldn't want to use one of those only to find that they don't like them!

4) THE CONTINUED GROWTH OF INSTANT MESSAGING

Most salespeople are used to using the phone and email for communication in sales. However, instant messaging is growing at a rapid rate. Whether that's using LinkedIn InMails or messages, using WhatsApp or even using text, it's a unique form of communication that needs to be understood.

Think back to the messaging section of this book; one of the poor examples of LinkedIn messaging that I shared was the 'Copy & Paste Email Message'. Some people are just using email style in instant messaging, which doesn't work.

Salespeople need to understand and learn how to use instant messaging effectively in sales. It's not an email, nor is it a text you'd send your best friend. It's something in between.

5) FUTURE BUYERS/YOUNGER GENERATIONS/MILLENNIALS

As the years go on, younger generations will continue to climb the career ladder and it won't be long before the majority of senior decision makers will consist of millennials and younger. These are generations that have been brought up with the internet, social media, instant messaging and video communication. These are generations that no longer had to (or wanted to) make phone calls. They want to communicate on their terms.

As salespeople and sales teams, we need to be ready for this continued shift. If your strategy hasn't changed in the last 10 years and is heavily reliant on cold calls, it is highly likely that you will struggle in the future.

Equally, sales teams need to start learning a wider breadth of platforms and tools.

6) NEW SOCIAL MEDIA NETWORKS

In this book I have shown you how to utilise LinkedIn, but there are other social networks that can be used as well, such as Facebook, Twitter and Instagram. New social networks are popping up all of the time; most don't last but some do. As salespeople our role is to make sure we utilise the tools and platforms that our customers use.

Learning and using LinkedIn is challenging for some salespeople and sales teams, as is learning anything new and unknown. Hopefully this book has helped make it easier for you, but you must also be prepared for newer social networks that may become a part of sales.

Be prepared to learn them, master them and utilise them in your approach.

7) 24/7 WORKING

A final thought for you is the concept of 24/7 working. Not that long ago, sales and business were a Monday-to-Friday, nine-to-five job. The only time you would ever stand a chance of reaching and speaking to a prospect or customer would be between those times.

That time has been and gone.

We now live in a 24/7 world.

Our prospects and customers are active and contactable 24 hours a day, seven days a week and social media makes it even easier. I've had inbound sales leads come at 03:00/04:00 in the morning and 22:00/23:00 at night, and during every hour in between.

Some of your prospects will check LinkedIn the moment they wake up and will check it the moment they go to bed (and again every moment in between).

CHAPTER 26

THE PROSPECTING MAZE

I think one of the best ways to illustrate prospecting in modern selling is to use a finger maze puzzle ...

You should have seen one of these maze puzzles before. Several doors go into the maze, but only one will lead to the end at the middle. You follow different paths with your finger or with a pen to try and get it right.

Now in our modern-day world, each of our prospects and customers sits in their own little maze. Even you, the reader, as a consumer and buyer, will sit in your own little maze.

Each door into the maze represents a method of communication. One door will represent the phone or cold-calling, one door will represent email, one social media, one face to face, you get the idea. As we all know with these puzzles, only one (or two) doors will lead to the middle, and in the modern-day prospecting maze, often only one or two doors will lead you to the prospect.

And this is what I call the modern-day prospecting maze!

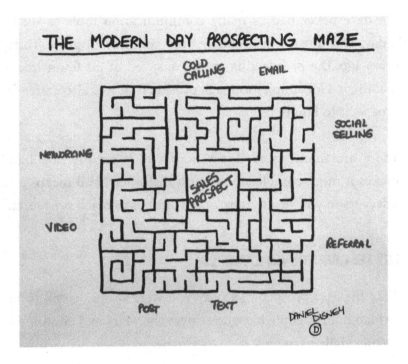

Now this is the important part …

EVERYONE IS DIFFERENT! Each maze around each individual prospect will be different. For some prospects, the door that will get you to the prospect in the middle will be the phone. For some prospects, the door that will get you to the prospect in the middle will be emailed. For some, it will be social media.

And this is the very crucial reality for sellers today.

We have never had as many communication tools as we do today, and those will probably only continue to grow. Thirty years ago, the prospecting maze consisted of far fewer doors, making it a lot simpler to reach prospects. It was also easier for prospects to ignore us.

There are many more doors now, which on the one hand makes it more complicated but on the other hand means as a salesperson you've got more opportunities to reach prospects.

LET ME GIVE YOU AN EXAMPLE ...

Take me as a prospect; let's say you were trying to sell to me (which many people have done over the years and continue to do on a daily basis).

If you were to go through the cold-calling door in my prospecting maze (in other words use cold-calling to try and sell to me), you would end up at a dead-end.

Personally, I don't answer cold-calls, even though I've spent years making them and years training and leading salespeople making them; as a buyer, it's not a method that I respond to. It doesn't matter how many times you try and call me; I won't answer.

I'm not alone in this; there are many people around the world, likely including many of your prospects, who don't answer cold-calls and will never answer cold-calls.

The reason this point is so important is that there are still so many companies out there where cold-calling is their only prospecting method. There are also companies where cold-calling is the core method alongside email.

If this is you, or your company, you're missing out on all of the prospects you could reach and sell to if you were to use other methods, such as LinkedIn and Social Selling.

Now as a salesperson, if you wanted to sell to me, let's say I was a huge prospect for you and one that you were so confident you could help, you would need to do something different.

Perhaps you'll connect with me via email, perhaps you'll see me at an event, but what will increase your chances is to connect and engage with me via LinkedIn.

The 'Modern Day Prospecting Maze' is there to help you understand the prospecting landscape out there now.

THE ABCS OF SOCIAL SELLING

Glengarry Glen Ross, featuring Alec Baldwin, created the popular sales phrase:

'Always Be Closing'

His speech to motivate the team to stop waiting around for sales and instead to focus on getting them to buy has helped plenty of sales professionals over the years. This was actually a very effective approach in the old age where selling required more push.

To be fair, closing sales is still a big part of sales success.

Unless you close the sale there is no sale; everything else means nothing until the deal is done. However, the way we close and in fact the way we sell has changed over the years.

Part of that change includes the introduction of social media into the sales process.

Social Selling is quite simply the effective use of social media in the sales process. Sales professionals can use social media to find, connect and communicate with prospects and customers in the same way they might use the phone, email or face to face.

With people now spending a lot of time on social media every day, it has become a crucial platform to help salespeople reach more people and enhance the way they sell.

There are key fundamentals to achieving success with social selling; a lot of salespeople spend a lot of time on social without generating many, if any, results. It's the same as those sales professionals who don't know how to cold-call effectively, making 100s of calls every day with no results at the end.

The key is to learn how to do it properly.

To help, here are the ABCs of Social Selling that focus on those core fundamentals:

1) Always Be CONNECTING

The first ABC of Social Selling is to Always Be Connecting. Effective social selling comes from your ability to find and connect with potential prospects and customers. The more prospects and customers that you have in your network, the more opportunities you'll be able to generate in the short and long term.

My Top Tip: There are many great methods that you can search for prospects on LinkedIn, but when actually connecting with people, it's often worth making the effort to your LinkedIn connection request. Nothing too sales-rich, just simple and light. To bring this tip to life set yourself a goal to connect with X amount of new people every single day. It could be five; it could be 10, whichever number works for you.

2) Always Be CREATING CONTENT

The second ABC is to Always Be Creating Content. Successful social sellers create engaging and great personal content to share with their network of prospects and customers. Their content helps showcase their expertise, build trust and start the all-important sales conversations.

My Top Tip: Your content shouldn't be about your product, but should be about YOU and your thoughts/knowledge/expertise. Create content such as posts, blogs, videos and images that offer value, insight, and knowledge, which will then draw people to your profile and website where you can then leverage that to start conversations.

3) Always Be (starting) CONVERSATIONS

One of the most important fundamentals and ABC Number 3 is Always Be (starting) Conversations. Social media is fun, likes and followers make us feel popular and important, but they certainly don't equate to pipeline and revenue until you turn them into REAL conversations that become meetings, pitches, and presentations.

My Top Tip: When you share great content, and you get likes and comments, use it to start a conversation via messenger. It might be a thank-you or an opportunity to discuss the topic further. Those conversations can then potentially be worked into sales conversations if they are a qualified prospect.

4) Always Be CONSISTENT

The last ABC is to Always Be Consistent. Social Selling success comes from it on a daily basis. For example, if you only cold-call someone once, and they don't answer, that's it. It's the same if you do some social activity but then don't for a period of time, the results won't come. You need to build it into your sales process and do it every day.

My Top Tip: Set time every single day to do social selling activities. It could be 15–30 minutes at the start of the day to connect with people, send messages and write a post.

You may then touch base at lunchtime to do the same, and again at the end of the day. Set your calendar to ensure that time is focused on social.

And there they are, my ABCs of Social Selling! Simple, but very powerful. Use them regularly and consistently and you'll start to see results before you know it.

NEXT STEPS

Now that you've read this book it's time to apply what you've learned! This will involve activities that you can action straight-away and others that you may want to add into your schedule and long-term strategy.

I would recommend starting with your profile. Make as many changes as you feel you need to, but get it to a place where you feel it makes the best possible impression for you.

After your profile, and if you work in sales right now, I'd then invest time in searching for and messaging prospects. Whilst doing this, and for anyone not in a sales targeted role, I'd also recommend then putting time into content and your personal brand.

As a final tip, and something you can do right now, I'd go into your calendar and set time each and every working day to invest in LinkedIn. It might be 15 minutes per day, it might be an hour, but book it in. This will help encourage you to start using it, and in time will make it a habit.

ACCESSING YOUR FREE LINKEDIN WEBINARS

As I have mentioned, my passion is helping people leverage LinkedIn to its full potential and so, along with writing this book, I wanted to give you the reader as much as I could to help you.

This is why for everyone who buys this book I'm also including eight hours of LinkedIn webinars that I have delivered to continue learning from. Along with reading this book, these will help you further your knowledge and learn more about how to get the most from LinkedIn.

To get access to these, simply email contact@thedailysales.net referencing the ISBN number on your book and they will be sent to you.

PLEASE LEAVE AN AMAZON REVIEW!

I genuinely hope you have enjoyed reading this book and that you're able to use it to generate more results from LinkedIn.

If you did enjoy it, I would be extremely grateful if you would spare five minutes to write a review on Amazon for it.

For everyone who takes the time to write one I would like to offer you an exclusive LinkedIn eBook pack for free as a thank-you!

This will include three LinkedIn training eBooks. All you need to do after leaving the review on Amazon is email a screenshot to contact@thedailysales.net and once verified the eBooks will be sent to you.

WORKING WITH DANIEL DISNEY

If you, your business or your sales team want to increase the amount of leads and sales that they're generating from LinkedIn, then Daniel is the man to call.

Whether it's to bring him to keynote at your next conference, company event or sales kick-off, deliver his one-day or two-day LinkedIn Masterclass or work on a coaching or consulting basis, you can find out more details on his website (www.danieldisney.online) or get in touch to enquire about availability.

LINKEDIN MASTERCLASS ONLINE COURSE

With over 60 LinkedIn training videos (over 10 hours), 35 guides, templates and scripts, 7 eBooks and several webinars, Daniel's on-demand LinkedIn Masterclass is one of the best online LinkedIn courses out there.

SPECIAL READER OFFER

As a thank-you for buying this book, you will be able to get an exclusive discount on the course. Full access is normally £499/$662, but you can join for just £99/$131! Simply use code OFFER99 to take advantage of this special price.

INTERNATIONAL KEYNOTE SPEAKER

Daniel Disney is also one of the most in-demand award winning sales speakers, bringing an unrivalled energy and passion to the stage, inspiring audiences around the world. Daniel lights up stages at Sales Kick-Offs, Corporate Sales Events, Expos and business conferences, as well as delivering highly engaging virtual talks and virtual keynotes, motivating and inspiring businesses, sales leaders and salespeople to leverage modern, social and digital sales tactics to improve and increase their sales.

'Dan lit up the stage, delivered an outstanding, power packed, keynote presentation, full of enthusiasm and passion about

the amazing potential when using LI properly for social selling. He explained the WHY? and the opportunity everyone was missing by not doing it, and he broke it down into easy to understand concepts for our global sales team and distribution partners, representing 35 countries'.

—*Jim Skelly VP International Sales at Cambro*

Daniel delivers a variety of talks on LinkedIn, Social Selling, Digital Selling, Personal Branding, Sales Motivation, Sales Leadership and more.

LINKEDIN & SOCIAL/DIGITAL TRAINING

Daniel Disney is one of the world's leading LinkedIn and social selling trainers. He helps businesses and sales teams leverage LinkedIn and social media to its full potential as a lead-generating and sales-generating machine.

His hugely popular 1-day and 2-day LinkedIn Masterclasses have been delivered to FTSE 500 companies and SMEs all around the world. It covers all aspects of social/digital selling, helping teams master LinkedIn and start generating more results from it.

Daniel also delivers Personal Branding Workshops and Content Masterclasses, as well as offering LIVE Virtual Training and an On-Demand Online LinkedIn Course.

LINKEDIN COACHING AND CONSULTING

Working with C-level executives, business owners, authors and experts, Daniel provides coaching and consulting, helping the top become the top on LinkedIn. Daniel provides his industry-leading 90-day LinkedIn programme, transforming personal brands, growing audiences and generating leads, as well as offering a monthly service to support long-term growth.

For more details head to www.danieldisney.online or to enquire about Daniel speaking at your next event or training you or your team, email danieldisney@thedailysales.net.

WHAT DANIEL'S CUSTOMERS SAY:

After reading Dan's book, I was so excited about everything he explained about social selling, that I bought 25 copies for our key sales managers.

I was convinced about Dan's best practices on social selling that he lays out perfectly in his book. Sending the book out to the sales team didn't get the 'buy in' or adoption that I was hoping for, so I hired Dan to give a 1-hour keynote speech at our 2020 International Sales Meeting that was held in January in the Philippines.

Dan lit up the stage, delivered an outstanding, power packed, keynote presentation, full of enthusiasm and passion about the amazing potential when using LI properly for social selling. He explained the WHY? and the opportunity everyone was missing by not doing it, and he broke it down into easy-to-understand concepts for our global sales team and distribution partners, representing 35 countries.

The 2nd day of the meeting Dan went deeper and taught 4 each, 1 hour, hands-on workshops to get everyone comfortable with the opportunity on LI. He successfully eliminated the fear factor, built the confidence and explained the ABCs of proper social selling, best practices, Do's and Don'ts and importance of taking consistent daily action. He was well worth the investment and I believe he convinced 120 international salespeople about getting on board with social selling. We will be hiring Dan again this summer to teach another class to our EMEA sales team so nobody backslides.

Jim Skelly Vice President of International Sales, Cambro Manufacturing

I cannot praise Daniel highly enough.

Daniel's Social Selling Masterclass was an extremely useful learning exercise for our team. He had extensive knowledge on possible techniques that could be applied to our business. And provided exceptionally detailed training and insight on social selling, which we were able to put into practice immediately.

Daniel's attitude and personality were exemplary. He displayed a good knowledge of the subject and built up a rapport with the attendees in no time. Daniel was a brilliant tutor, excellent quality of delivery, depth of knowledge and also communicated really well with all delegates. Pacing, delivery, passion for the subject and level of knowledge were/are excellent.

Our team thoroughly enjoyed this course and learned a great deal from the day spent at our HQ.

We thought the Masterclass was worth every penny and will certainly use him again.

Thank you again, Daniel, and keep up the great work you're doing in this space.

Tim Johnson – CSO at Visualsoft

Daniel spent the day with our sales, marketing, product, and IT team and delivered his LinkedIn training course, which was even better than I anticipated! Daniel connects with his audience, tailors his content to suit and even managed to perfectly engage a US team member who attended via video chat.

Daniel's knowledge, experience, and overall approach works impeccably well. I would recommend Daniel to anyone wanting to understand the power of social and I'd encourage you NOT to reserve his expertise to just sales as 'everyone works in sales!'

Luke Warren – Chief Executive Officer at Kinetic

If Social selling is your game, then Daniel Disney is the name you need to know!! A fantastically engaging and insightful workshop, Daniel really knows how to help you get the most from it!

Every member of our team got something worthwhile from it and within days we have all been trying new techniques and venturing into the seemingly scary world of Blogs and Vlogs (it's not as scary as it first seems!).

I cannot rate Daniel's workshop highly enough and it is a must for anybody looking to improve their social media performance.

Gavin Dawson – Managing Director at CamAce Ltd

I would thoroughly recommend Daniel and his sessions on social selling. I recently attended one of his sessions and since then have seen a huge improvement on my use of social media.

After a few tentative attempts at interesting and engaging posts I seemed to hit a note with people and had over 4,000 views on a simple picture. I don't have anywhere near 4,000 connections. My profile views jumped by over 700% and have had many connection requests.

Graham Cameron – Barclay Communications

I recently attended Daniel's 'Social Selling Masterclass'. Daniel has been there, seen it, done it! and his workshop was excellent, with his incredible experience and insights shared alongside dispelling some common myths about social media selling.

Daniel's enthusiasm, energy and experience were apparent during the day. I have implemented the learnings and results are coming in (on some prospects that I've been targeting for over 9 months!) ....

If you get the chance to attend this workshop, you will not regret the investment. Daniel is one of the best social media experts I've had the pleasure of meeting and working with.

Ian Beighton – Senior Vice President Business Development and Sales EMEA at Innovecs

I first met Daniel at the Sales Innovation Expo and had the pleasure of working with him as he was a Keynote Speaker for my show and his Keynote was one of the most attended of the show.

His dedication and diligence to his profession is a testament to the company he has built from scratch. I feel I have learned a lot from him in regard to Social Selling and look at him as being at the forefront of the 'Social Selling Revolution'.

Gavin Harris – Director of B2B Marketing Expo

ACKNOWLEDGEMENTS

There is a great quote:

'If the people around you don't lift you up, then you don't have a circle of friends, you have a cage'.

—Unknown

I am very fortunate to have amazing people around me who have helped me throughout my life, and I work hard to make sure I surround myself with the best people that I can. I'd like to acknowledge them as being influential in everything I do now and in writing this book.

Firstly, I want to thank my amazing partner, Laurie. I wouldn't be who I am today or be doing what I do if it wasn't for you.

Laurie helped me years ago and keeps my ego in check. Working and being successful in sales, and entering the world of social media, can have a huge impact on your ego. Laurie has helped me remember what's important in life and the importance of keeping grounded. Whilst it is important to celebrate success and be proud of your achievements, success isn't a destination, it's a journey.

I would like to say a big thank-you to our two wonderful sons as well, Joshua and Lewis. Everything I do, I do for you both. To try and provide you with opportunities that I didn't have, to provide you with experiences and memories, to help as much as I physically can to set up a good future for you. I am so immensely proud of the men you are both becoming and thank you for being a constant source of motivation for me.

I'd also like to say thank-you to my nan and grandad, two of the biggest inspirations in my life. They taught me the importance of hard work and determination, and the importance of family. I spent a lot of my childhood with them and they were the centrepiece of our family. They worked so hard throughout their lives to provide for their children and their grandchildren. Every day I work hard to build a future for my family as they did for theirs.

To my dad, who taught me both humour and creativity. My dad is the best artist that I know, and pushed me to be creative as often as I can. He also has the best sense of humour, and bringing those together with my passion for sales helped me create and build The Daily Sales.

To my mum, you would listen to me as a child talk about my many dreams of starting my own businesses and being success-ful. You listened, you challenged and you guided me.

To my Uncle Al and Auntie Kim, you have always pushed me to be the best I can. Uncle Al, you will always be the person who guided me into sales and supported me through my early sales roles. I wouldn't have achieved the success I have in sales were it not for you.

To my sister, Yasmin, you've always inspired me to dream big but to always have fun along the way. No matter what, you've always been there as I will always be for you.

To Nikki and Geoff, you took me into the family from day one and have been supportive and guiding in helping me achieve my dreams of building my business. Thank you for being there for me, Laurie, the boys, and thank you for the holidays and roasts.

To my best friend, Croly. Your entrepreneurial aspirations inspired me when we were just 16 and running our own little eBay businesses. We've shared successes, failures, laughs and many, many memories.

Thank you as well to Annie and the team at Wiley for all of your support and help during the writing of this book.

I'd also like to say a big thank-you to the amazing people I'm honoured to have in my professional circle, as my peers, colleagues and friends: Chris Murray, Dale Dupree, Alex Goldfayn, Gavin Ingham, Steve Burton, Karen Dunne-Squire, Darryl Praill, Benjamin Dennehey, Devin Reed, Niraj Kapur, Alison Edgar, Stu Heinecke, Scott Barker, Mark Jung, Paul Fifield, Ben Wright, Jim Skelly, Jeb Blount, Tony J Hughes, Will Barron, Holly Tripp, Tyler Lessard, Zoe Pepper, Lee Bartlett, Tony Goodchild, James Ski, Ian Gribble, Tony Morris, Vedran & Mirela, Scott McNicholas, Nazma Qurban, Ed Armishaw, Shane Burchett, and everyone else that I can't fit in (but who hopefully know who they are!).

Finally, thank you to YOU, the reader.

Thank you for buying this book and thank you for reading it. I not only hope you enjoyed it, but that it helps you get more from LinkedIn.

Please feel free follow me on LinkedIn & Twitter for regular content on LinkedIn, Social Selling and Sales:

LinkedIn: https://uk.linkedin.com/in/danieldisney
Twitter: @thedandisney

If you have any questions at all, please feel free to email me at contact@thedailysales.net.

Happy Social Selling!

Daniel Disney

INDEX

INDEX